THE STEW COOKBOOK

By Johnrae Earl and James McCormick

PRICE / STERN / SLOAN

Publishers, Inc., Los Angeles

Stew's on!

-An old cowboy cry

STEW FROM THE DARK AGES — AND BEFORE

A delightful excerpt from a *Fastnachtspiel,* or Shrovetide play, from 15th Century Germany goes like this:

"And God said, 'Let the earth bring forth the living creature after his kind, cattle, and creeping thing, and beasts of the earth after his kind,' and it was so. And God made the beast of the earth after his kind, and cattle after their kind, and everything that creepeth and groweth upon the earth after his kind, and He put all into a pot and boiled it after the pot's own kind. And on the seventh day God ended His work that He had made, and He rested from all his work which He had made. And He supped from the pot on what the pot had made, and it was good, and He called it stew."

And there it is, in a steal from the story of creation in the book of Genesis, all mashed together like potatoes in a crock — the origin of the dish we call stew, its link with divinity, and the complete gastronomical satisfaction this classic fare provides.

But where did stew really originate? Is it true that "Mulligan's Stew" was invented by a bum? Is "Cannibal Stew" a racist slur against Africa or is there such a thing? When is a gelatinous consistency to a stew desirable, and when a watery one? What about free-expression stew as against stew made by clearly defined rules and recipes?

The Stew Cookbook will answer these questions and many more. In addition, it will provide more than one hundred recipes for making stews, grouped under the general classifications of beef stews; lamb, mutton, and veal stews; fish and seafood stews; vegetarian stews; stews made with fowl; and wild game stews. To these the authors have added gourmet stews, strange stews, and stews collected from around the world.

All of the recipes have been kitchen-tested and judged excellent. If the definition of "stew" is that it is "a meal unto itself cooked in one pot," then all — with the rare exception of a Carbonnades a la Flammande (boiled potatoes are served on the side with this one so that the beer sauce the beef stew is cooked in can be fully appreciated) — are genuine stews. In *The Stew Cookbook* you are guaranteed not to find any soups, hashes, or chowders.

'Let them eat stew!'

Actually, stew, unlike a Hershey bar or an Eskimo Pie, did not need to be invented. Human beings just took to it naturally once fire sprang from a flint spark and utensils were devised to withstand the heat. It was known in the second Chinese period, the Chou dynasty, a thousand years before Christ. Before that, there is evidence of a pot boiling and figures carrying animals, vegetables, and green leaves to the pot, in the slogans, signs, advertisements, popular songs, and menus cavemen and women scribbled on their damp walls. Some Greek pottery, especially those unearthed from the Stone Age in Crete and North Greece, tell the same story. So stew can be assumed to be a quite natural evolvement of man's instinct to survive in a world that has always been hostile to him.

There is no dish that is as perfect a meal as stew. It is well within reach of everybody's talent to make — and pocketbook to afford. And if one is to believe the great French chef Escoffier, it is the healthiest meal one can eat. It is a sort of percolating pot of energy and stamina. Stew tends to communalize the diners who are sharing it, bringing forth all that is gregarious and good-natured in the inner man. Yet nothing in the culinary world is so maligned.

For some obscure reason, many otherwise excellent cookbooks do not list a stew. "Ragouts" and "goulashes," perhaps, but no stew. This is tantamount to saying that stews do not exist. "Stew is a poor man's dish," say many gourmets, who should know better. In New York City and London, both of which boast the most diversified restaurant fare in the world, there are no "Stew Joints," as there are "Chili Joints" or "Hamburger Joints."

Although Oxtail Ragout was created for the rich, it is rarely served any more at fashionable dinner parties. The reason is, because the host or hostess is afraid guests do not like to use their fingers to nibble off the best of the meat that clings to the bone. Beef stew likewise, in spite of the fact that it is a perfect dish for large private parties — it can be stretched quite far, it can be prepared in advance and reheated, it can continue cooking or be kept hot waiting for late arrivals, and it can be dressed up to rival any dish labeled "haute cuisine."

Marie Antoinette might just as well have cried, "Let them eat stew!" and she would have been understood and just as unceremoniously guillotined, so contemptuously do we regard this classic and always delectable dish.

Some discipline, please!

Stew is not, as many people — especially in the southwestern United States and some parts of the Midwest — believe, an "anything goes" dish. Making a stew with any combination of ingredients you happen to find on the kitchen shelf or in the vegetable bin is a short cut ending up at a blank wall.

The gospel of some stew lovers that stews are not made but thrown together thus needs drastic revision. *The Stew Cookbook* is a start in that direction.

Escoffier believed that the disciplining of stew-making was necessary for any culture which prided itself on its cuisine, and that it was from the repression of the free-form impulse in stew-making that the power of the stew was built. The Belgian chef, Sti Beauchard, here agrees for once with Escoffier. Beauchard does not forget that without the stew discipline which the so-called free-expressionists have forced upon us since time began, there would be nothing more in our cuisine than stew created by African tribesmen, and maybe less. (Here Beauchard shows his ignorance of Africa. Africans have some delicious stews in great variety. Ghana alone has twenty different kinds, of which Ntraba Forae, or Garden Egg Stew, is unequalled.)

There would be neither Lamb Stew Piquante nor any of the skills and knowledge which have created the present stew world without discipline. There would also not be the problem of the stew bum who will eat anything that has boiled in a pot for hours! Stew authorities tend to forget this fact quite naively, committed as they are to their poetic or moralizing passion for free expression in cooking, which too often alienates them from the true nature of the "facts of life" about stew, and stew's complex links with economy, society, and culture.

Of course, we can forgive a Belgian chef his fatuity when he is speaking about food. But it is the view of the authors of *The Stew Cookbook* that there does indeed come a point when the cult of "formless" stew destroys stew, undermines one's passion for it, and blots out awareness of the countless subtleties and varieties of taste to be found in stews.

The technologically efficient cook, with his pressure cooker and best cuts of meat, defeated in the contradiction that is stew making and stew enjoyment, is ultimately the one who cannot make a stew that draws a cry of "More!" from his guests. In the matter of stew-making, he is impotent. He has lost the power to discipline himself; he does not know what he is doing. At this point, technology diminishes facility and demolishes stew. Ingredients no longer are an enlargement of the stew, but a substitute for it, and repress and frustrate stew enjoyment.

Let's dispense with Mr. Mulligan

The most reckless free-form stew-maker of all time was Mr. Paddy Mulligan. He was an owlish-eyed, mighty-mouthed geyser of a man who reigned as king of the hoboes along the Pennsylvania Railroad line from about 1916 to 1924. Also, he invented Mulligan's Stew, alas!

During Paddy's famous years he "rode the rods" — the connecting members under old time freight cars — on the Penn's mainline between Bryn Mawr, Pennsylvania, and Alliance, Ohio, and he was well-known in every jail from Altoona to Girard, Ohio, and in Alliance.

Eating was always a hit-and-miss affair for Paddy and his band of bums, since they would work only when forced to. It thus fell to Paddy to raise the eating standards of hoboes to new heights and set the art of stew-making back to the Dark Ages. That was when he introduced his Mulligan's Stew to his pals.

Every Mulligan Stew was different. The recipe of the day depended on what Paddy and his friends could promote or steal. If lucky, they would bum a piece of beef. Then they would scrounge through the fields for whatever vegetables were easy pickings.

The next step was so natural it was practically Cro-Magnon. Firewood was lined up and a sheltered spot for the feast was found — usually in a bridge underpass. Then they would hunt up an old can — any one that didn't leak would do. After filling the pot with water from a nearby stream and getting it to a rolling boil, in went the meat and vegetables and in an hour or two — if the law didn't interfere — the Mulligan Stew was ready.

Chicken sometimes ended up in the pot instead of beef. Paddy and his cronies had some close calls with chicken stew. He once told a nosy policeman, "Poddon me, sir, but that little old chicken just flew into our pot." Which must have satisfied the cop, because he replied, "Thas orright," and left.

Mulligan and his gang traveled lightly, of course. They rarely had oregano, basil, thyme, or even salt and pepper in the belongings wrapped in bandanas they carried over their shoulders. The original Mulligan Stew, therefore, depended on onions or carrots and whatever other vegetables were available for its flavor.

So for those of you who are believers in the "free-form" style of stew-making — or incidentally are apt to romanticize Mulligan's carefree way of life — here is an original Mulligan Stew recipe for you to try.

Go ahead and cook it over your next campfire or on your kitchen range, and as you eat it, you may picture yourself around a hoboe's campfire somewhere on the outskirts of a Pennsylvania town.

The rest of us will go on to stews that are really stews.

MULLIGAN STEW

2 pounds round steak, cut into 2-inch chunks or
1 2½ pound chicken, cut up
2 carrots, cut into 2-inch slices
2 medium-sized onions, sliced
5 medium-sized potatoes, sliced

Put round steak or chicken pieces into a pot and cover the contents with water. Simmer half an hour, then add the vegetables. Simmer another half an hour, or until meat and vegetables are tender.

If you are a "salt and pepper everything" family, you may, if you like, add salt and pepper to taste. Also, if you want a thicker stew, mix one tablespoon flour with a bit of cold water and stir it into the stew. Simmer until it reaches the consistency you desire.

It is now ready to serve to your "hoboes."

BASIC STEWS

Stew Tasters International (S.T.I.) is a society of looney Chicago newspapermen and saloon owners, with some doctors and lawyers thrown in, whose chief interest in life is in raising the poor man's dish of stew to the level of international stature they think it deserves.

The society is not as provincial as it sounds; it honors the Belgian chef mentioned in the previous chapter, Sti Beauchard, the man it credits with making — out of the many forms of Belgium's favorite stew, Carbonnades a la Flammande — the one recipe usually followed in many of the finest restaurants in Europe (Beauchard's recipe will be found on page 100).

Although usually wrapped in the smell of after-dinner cigars and befogged by booze, the society scores a point now and then by producing a new recipe for stew that even a French restaurant could feature. Well-traveled and some of them very well-heeled, the society members carry pamphlets of recipes wherever their duties or their pleasures might take them and like missionaries, drop them off at dining places where they stop. To date, nobody knows how many restaurant owners they have influenced. It's all been in good will and fellowship, and spreaders of the faith have never paused to count their disciples, anyway.

That said, it should come as no surprise to learn that the society ranks plain American beef stew, with its heritage of less than one hundred and fifty years, among the best stews the world has created. What else would you expect saloon owners and a bunch of rowdy newspapermen to say?

Still, the society has a good point. The basic stew in the United States is beef stew. There may be pork, lamb, veal, and oyster stew, but beef stew is king. Beef stew diversified. American beef stew is laced more generously with meat than any other stew. Its variations are almost endless because beef goes well with any vegetable where most other meats, and certainly fish, do not. Finally, it's a dish that knows no class boundaries, being suitable served as a meal in itself in restaurants, or on the tables in the poorest homes.

Combinations of meat and vegetables for main dishes have been popular all over the world since time began, of course, and each is distinct from the others. That distinction generally is in the combination of ingredients, flavorings, treatment of foodstuffs, and the varieties of vegetables used.

Irish stew with its mixture of mutton, potatoes, and onions is a far cry indeed from Poland's teeming Bigos, a stew made with sour cabbage, beef, apples, and tomato puree. Likewise, vastly different, are Denmark's Gule Arter with flour dumplings and forcemeat (ground beef or chicken balls *forced* through a grinder) added, and India's many-vegetable Chankee, a curry stew.

It remained for Americans, however, to devise their national stew at about the same time the breeding and rearing of cattle-primarily-to-supply-meat became a modern development. Formerly known as oxen, cattle from ancient times had been used as draft animals and for supplying milk. They were utilized as food ultimately, but this was secondary, and among many peoples their flesh was regarded, for religious or other reasons, as unfit for humans to consume.

Then came the development of the Angus, Hereford, and Polled Hereford strains, mostly in Scotland and England, and with their sweet meat and high palatability, beef came of age. And America, with its vast grazing lands, quickly became beef country, a title it has never relinquished.

Today about two-thirds of the billion head of cattle that roam the earth at any one time are in Europe, Asia, and Africa. But it is the United States which is by far the largest producer of exportable beef and veal — about one-third of the world's supply.

So it's no surprise then that stew made with chunks of beef lavishly strewn through it should be the American contribution to this ancient culinary feast.

In this chapter you will find recipes for the best beef stew in the land. Experts will quarrel over them. S.T.I. members will tear out the pages and use them as targets for darts of contempt in the saloons where they meet. Nevertheless, these same experts will know, deep down, that these recipes both encompass and surpass the whole range of slap-dash stews ever devised, and serve to give form to what up to now has been utter chaos in the American stew world.

Here are some points to remember in making stews:

- Do not overcook. This makes the meat stringy and hard to chew.
- Never let a stew boil, it toughens the meat. The temperature should be held at a point which permits the stew to bubble a bit, but never go into a galloping boil.
- When freezing leftover stew, the pieces of meat, vegetables, and other solid ingredients should be completely covered by the sauce. The stew should be cool but not cold when you are ready to freeze it.
- When reheating frozen stew, it would be best for the container used in freezing to be placed in a pan of boiling water. Otherwise, remove the stew to a saucepan and gently reheat it, stirring frequently to prevent sticking. Frozen stews sometimes require a little more liquid when they are being reheated.

Now, let's get on to stew-making!

DUTCH COLONIAL *(Serves 5)*

Governor Kieft of New York opened New York's first tavern in Dutch Colonial days.

2 pounds chuck steak, cut into 1-inch cubes
1 teaspoon salt
½ teaspoon black pepper
3 tablespoons flour
4 tablespoons bacon drippings
 (or cooking oil)
1 clove garlic, minced
1 medium onion, sliced thin
2 tablespoons parsley, chopped
1 rib celery, chopped

1 bay leaf, crumbled
3 cups chicken broth (or 4 chicken bouillon cubes dissolved in 3 cups boiling water)
1 cup dry red wine
6 small white onions, peeled
6 carrots, cut into 3-inch pieces
6 medium potatoes, quartered
2 tablespoons cornstarch, mixed with ¼ cup cold water

Mix the salt, pepper and flour together and toss meat cubes into the mixture until they are coated. Heat the bacon drippings in a heavy kettle. Add the minced garlic and brown the meat slightly. Add the sliced onion, parsley, celery, bay leaf, bouillon, and wine. Bring to a boil. Reduce heat, cover kettle, and simmer slowly two hours, or until the meat is tender. Add the whole white onions, carrots, and potatoes one and a half hours after stew starts simmering. When the vegetables are tender, stir in the cornstarch and simmer until the stew begins to thicken. Serve hot.

(Serves 5) BOSTON COMMONS

In spite of their rich fisheries and plentiful game, the people of Massachusetts always have been hearty beef eaters. Here is one of their stew recipes that goes back to Abolitionist days.

2 pounds chuck, cut into 1½-inch cubes
½ cup flour
4 tablespoons butter
1 tablespoon olive oil
2 teaspoons salt
¼ teaspoon black pepper
½ teaspoon celery salt
¼ teaspoon thyme
1 clove garlic, minced

2 cups water
1 tablespoon Worcestershire sauce
2 tablespoons bottled chili sauce
5 medium potatoes, quartered
1 can (16 ounces) cooked white onions
10 whole cloves
1 package (10 ounces) frozen peas and carrots

Toss meat cubes in flour and coat well. Save the leftover flour. Heat butter and olive oil in a large kettle. Add meat and brown lightly on all sides and set aside. Add salt, pepper, celery salt, thyme, garlic, and remaining flour to the kettle. Stir in water, and bring to boil. Reduce heat and simmer until mixture thickens.

Return the meat to the kettle and stir in Worcestershire sauce and chili sauce. Simmer, covered, for one hour. Add potatoes and the liquid from the canned onions. Stick cloves into one onion and add along with other onions to pot. Cook thirty more minutes (until potatoes are almost tender). Add the package of peas and carrots and simmer fifteen minutes more. Remove onions with cloves before serving.

CHUCK WAGON *(Serves 6)*

The age of beef began, and cowboys from Texas started carving out trails to the north. On every cattle drive, the chuck wagon brought up the rear. And here is the type of stew those wagons served the boys.

2 pounds chuck, cut into 2-inch cubes
3/4 cup flour
4 tablespoons butter
1 cup water
4 carrots, chopped
2 medium onions, chopped

1 can (1 pound, 13 ounces) tomatoes
1 teaspoon pepper
2 cloves garlic, minced
1½ teaspoons celery salt
2 teaspoons salt
1 can (20 ounces) lima beans

Dredge meat cubes in flour to coat all sides. Heat butter in a large kettle and then lightly brown beef on all sides. Stir in the water and scrape the bottom of the kettle with a spatula. Add carrots, onions, tomatoes, garlic, celery salt, pepper, and salt. Bring to a boil. Reduce heat, cover kettle, and simmer forty-five minutes, or until meat is tender. Stir in lima beans. Heat through and serve.

RANCHER

A time-honored and extremely healthy dish is this cabbage-laden variation of Chuck Wagon stew. It still is served in many homes throughout the west.

2½ pounds chuck steak, cut into 2-inch cubes
½ cup lard
2 cups water
1 teaspoon pepper
1 tablespoon salt

2 teaspoons paprika
6 carrots, cut into 1-inch pieces
3 medium onions, sliced
6 medium potatoes, diced
4 ribs celery, chopped
½ head cabbage, shredded

Heat the lard to sizzling in a large kettle and then brown meat on all sides. Stir in the water, pepper, salt, and paprika, and cover and simmer forty-five minutes, or until meat is tender. Add carrots, onions, potatoes, and celery and simmer until potatoes are tender. Add cabbage and simmer ten more minutes, and serve.

CHURCH SERVICE *(Serves 6)*

Small towns people in the Midwest were not idle as the nation's stew pots simmered. Here is one for a Sunday afternoon that Great Grandmother could put in the oven while she went to church.

2 pounds chuck, cut into 1½-inch cubes
1 tablespoon salt
½ cup flour
4 tablespoons butter
1 tablespoon cooking oil
1 teaspoon pepper
2 cups (16 ounces) canned tomatoes
3 ribs celery, chopped
1 small green pepper, diced

2 medium onions, diced
1 teaspoon sweet basil
1 teaspoon tarragon
1 clove garlic, minced
6 medium potatoes, quartered
1 can (16 ounces) mushroom caps
3 tablespoons flour, mixed with
½ cup cold water

Mix one teaspoon of salt with flour and dredge meat pieces in it, coating all sides. Heat butter and oil in a large kettle and lightly brown the meat. Add remaining salt along with the pepper, tomatoes, celery, green pepper, onions, basil, tarragon, garlic, and potatoes. Add water to cover and stir to blend well. Cover and cook for two hours in a preheated 325-degree oven.

At the end of this time add the mushrooms and stir in the flour-water mixture over open flame on top of stove. Cover, return to oven, and cook ten more minutes. Serve hot.

(Serves 4) HELL'S KITCHEN

New York, meanwhile, was seething. Hordes of immigrants were pouring in and bringing their own likes and dislikes to stew. This one is from an old recipe found in Hell's Kitchen when it was thronging with Italians.

1 pound ground round steak
1 tablespoon olive oil
1 small green pepper, chopped
1 medium onion, chopped fine
2 teaspoons salt

½ teaspoon pepper
1 clove garlic, minced
1 can (1 pound 12 ounces) tomatoes
1 cup uncooked elbow macaroni
½ cup parmesan cheese, grated

Get oil hot in a large, heavy skillet. Brown meat, stirring with a fork to break it up. Stir in the green pepper, onion, salt, pepper, garlic, tomatoes (with juice), and macaroni. Stir to blend. Cover skillet tightly and simmer twenty minutes until macaroni is just tender. Stir occasionally to keep macaroni from sticking. Stir in cheese, heat through, and serve immediately.

PENNSYLVANIA DUTCH *(Serves 6)*

This stew is remembered from childhood around Mahonington, Pennsylvania, which proves that the German and Dutch newcomers were busy at it, too.

2½ pounds boneless beef, cut into 2-inch cubes
3 tablespoons butter
2 large onions, sliced thin
1 teaspoon salt
1 teaspoon paprika
3 ripe tomatoes, chopped fine
1 cup water
4 potatoes, sliced
6 ounces stale beer

Heat butter in a large pot or Dutch oven and sauté onions just until they begin to soften. Add beef cubes and sauté three minutes, stirring occasionally. Blend in salt and paprika. Add tomatoes and water. Cover and place in a preheated 325-degree oven for one hour. Add potato slices and more water, if needed, and cook until potatoes are tender. Stir in beer, heat through, and serve.

(Serves 4) POTLUCK STEW

The "anything goes" cooks were on the rise, and stew began taking on the hodge-podge character it still retains today. This one, however, is one of the best we've seen, principally because of the clever way it utilizes leftovers.

1 pound leftover cooked beef, lamb, or pork
2 tablespoons butter
1 medium onion, chopped
½ cup dry white wine
1 tablespoon tomato sauce
½ teaspoon pepper
1 teaspoon salt
Cooked rice for 4 persons

Cut leftover meat into cubes and set to one side. Heat butter in a large skillet and sauté the onion until it is soft. Add wine, tomato sauce, salt, and pepper. Cover and simmer ten minutes. Add meat cubes and simmer ten more minutes.

Divide rice into four serving dishes and pour meat and sauce over it, and serve.

MODERN TIMES *(Serves 5 or 6)*

No history of stew in America could be complete without a "quickie" stew. And here is a very good one.

3 slices bacon, diced
3 large onions, chopped
1 clove garlic, minced
2 pounds round steak, sliced
into very thin strips

1 teaspoon salt
¼ teaspoon black pepper
½ teaspoon marjoram
1 cup dry white wine
2 cups sour cream

Sauté bacon in large skillet until it is almost crisp. Add garlic and onions and sauté until onion is soft, not brown. Add meat strips and sauté two minutes, stirring frequently. Transfer meat and onions to a pot or a Dutch oven and sprinkle with salt, pepper, and marjoram. Pour wine into skillet and scrape bottom of skillet with spatula. Pour into pot with the meat. Bring to boil. Reduce heat, cover, and simmer thirty minutes. Stir in sour cream, one spoonful at a time. Heat through and serve.

VEAL, LAMB, AND MUTTON STEWS

Ever since Thomas Pynchon drove a herd of cattle from Springfield, Massachusetts, to Boston in the spring of 1655 to start the New World's fat cattle industry, Americans traditionally have been heavy beef eaters.

Not for us were the dog, sheep, or horse, yak, llama, and donkey which some societies, even today, carry over from their Stone and Bronze Age ancestors. Young dog meat might have been sweet and tender, and so might horse and donkey, when Caveman Gurd was battling everything in his environment just to stay alive. But as mankind progressed from the discovery of fire and started settling into his fixed community habits, the dog, horse, and donkey became loving companions and sturdy working tools and so gradually were divorced from the carnivorous appetites of Gurd's ancestors.

Not so lucky were sheep, which early became a symbol of spring, with its flesh popular at religious festivals – particularly the Christian Easter and the Jewish Passover – and almost everywhere in the biblical belt along the Mediterranean.

But not in America, where sheep might as well have gone on producing wool until they were slaughtered for their hides, and the meat exported to Britain as mutton, for all the natives seemed to care. Lamb just wasn't our kind of meat.

Even today, America ranks behind New Zealand, Argentina, Australia, and Uruguay in sheep export, with a mere 10,000 tons annually compared to New Zealand's 260,000 tons.

Why lamb and mutton have never curried much favor with Americans as they have with our cousins, the British – or veal, either, for that matter, which is consumed in far greater quantities in France and middle Europe than here – is explainable by psychology as well as economics and taste.

In the early stories of the Wild West which spread across the continent and fertilized the imaginations of the colonizing mechanics, artisans, shopkeepers, and teachers back east, the romantic cowboys driving their herds of cattle through Indian territory from Texas to Kansas and Missouri, always were the "good guys" and the sheep ranchers the "bad guys."

Zane Grey's popular novels of the west culminated the era and are the definitive works of the genre.

The persuasiveness of these stories of robust and wide-ranging cowboys fighting the uptight sheepmen for grazing land was subliminal and strong. Lamb meat took on an increasingly bad taste and odor. To enhance that, generations of American children grew up with T. Fleet's *Songs for the Nursery, or Mother Goose's Melodies for Children* (Boston, 1719), which included Mary and her lamb with fleece as white as snow, and Mary's lamb was not an object to be butchered. Children's stories, Christmas tree decorations, kindergarten cutouts, and toy lambs resting with baby in its crib, all tended to anthropomorphize lambs and make them part of the family. American English is the only language in the world with an endearing term for the lamb, "lambkin," which is always used as a term of affection.

As for veal, Americans like their meat blood red, aged ten to fourteen days, and marbled with fat (which exerts an internal basting effect on the meat while it is cooking). Veal calves are fed on milk and a high protein calf meal, and no green or leaflike food is permitted. The consequent iron deficiency produces a whitish color to the meat, and that, as the saying goes, "ain't he-man" enough for Americans.

Too bad. If it were otherwise, the first law of Economics I would take over: production would increase and prices would decline. As it is now, whenever demand for lamb and veal inches upward, so does the price; as the price rises, demand decreases. And both meats are trapped in a very limited economic curve.

Yet beef calves and sheep are highly nutritious, and both lend that important variety to animal meat diets that invigorate the spirit as well as the body. Veal is in fact higher in protein than beef, and lower in fat. Lamb is higher in food energy than either veal or beef. In all other vitamins and minerals found in beef, both veal and lamb compare quite favorably.

So here is a chapter on stews that will enable you to take advantage of all that nutrition, no matter what the price for the meat is. Stews use the cheaper cuts; even the neck and scrag of the lamb may be used. Generally it is the shoulder, though, or, in the case of leftovers, a second meal from a leg of lamb.

CHESTNUTS 'N' STUFF *(Serves 4)*

Talk about a healthy meal! In addition to veal, this one is rich in nuts, which are high in the zinc and magnesium that tend to be deficient in the average diet, especially since galvanized pipes, pots, and pans have fallen into disuse.

2 pounds boneless stewing veal, cut into 2-inch cubes
½ stick butter
1½ tablespoons flour
2 cups water
1 teaspoon salt
½ teaspoon thyme
¼ teaspoon pepper

½ pound small white onions, peeled
½ pound chestnuts, peeled
1 tablespoon flour
1 tablespoon lemon juice
1 egg yolk
¼ cup half and half
¼ cup dry white wine
2 tablespoons parsley, minced

Melt butter in a large skillet or Dutch oven and brown the veal cubes lightly on all sides. Sprinkle the meat with a little flour and stir in water, salt, thyme, and pepper. Bring the pot to simmering. Cover and let cook gently for thirty minutes. Add onions and chestnuts and simmer thirty minutes more, or until meat and onions are tender. Mix 1 tablespoon flour, lemon juice, egg yolk, half and half, and wine together and stir into the stew. Cook until stew begins to thicken. Garnish with parsley and serve.

(Serves 5 or 6) LAST MINUTE PEAS

The trick in cooking, besides washing dishes and utensils as you use them, is to save yourself as much work as possible so that you get to the table fresh enough to enjoy what you've made. So why shell peas when frozen ones are just as good, and often better?

2 pounds veal shoulder,
cut into 2-inch cubes
3/4 cup flour
2 teaspoons salt
3/4 teaspoon black pepper
2 slices bacon, minced
6 small onions, quartered

1 pound fresh yellow beans,
cut into 2-inch lengths
3 ribs celery, cut into 2-inch lengths
1 medium green pepper, cut into rings
1 can (16 ounces) tomatoes
1 package frozen peas

Put flour, salt, and pepper into a paper bag. Add veal cubes and shake well to coat all sides.

Saute minced bacon in a large, heavy skillet until it is almost crisp. Add veal and sauté until golden brown on all sides. Transfer meat to stewing pot and add onions, beans, celery, green pepper, and tomatoes. Cover pot tightly and place in a preheated 350-degree oven. Cook for one and a half hours. Remove cover from the pot the last twenty minutes of cooking and then, five minutes before stew is done, stir in the frozen peas and serve hot.

MARY'S LAMB *(Serves 6)*

Nothing but the best should be made out of this adorable creature, and this is the most interesting lamb stew ever created.

2 pounds lamb shoulder,
cut into 2-inch cubes
3/4 cup flour
2 teaspoons salt
3/4 teaspoon black pepper
3 slices lean bacon, diced
2 cloves garlic, minced
2 medium-sized onions, chopped
3 ribs celery, chopped fine
1 carrot, scraped and chopped

½ pound fresh mushrooms, cleaned
and sliced into thirds
1 cup uncooked rice
3 ripe tomatoes, chopped
1 bay leaf, crumbled
½ teaspoon oregano
½ teaspoon basil
2 chicken bouillon cubes, dissolved
in 1 cup boiling water
1 cup dry white wine
1 tablespoon fresh parsley, chopped

Put flour, salt and black pepper into a paper bag. Add lamb and shake. Sauté bacon in skillet until almost crisp. Add lamb and brown.

Transfer meat to a large pot. Put garlic, chopped onions, celery, carrot and mushrooms into skillet and sauté in the bacon fat five minutes. Place the vegetables in the pot and add rice, tomatoes, bay leaf, oregano and basil. Heat chicken bouillon in skillet, then scrape bottom of skillet. Pour bouillon into meat pot. Add wine and stir.

Cover pot and place in a 325-degree oven for one hour, or until rice has absorbed most of the liquid. Add salt and pepper if needed. Sprinkle with parsley, and serve hot.

Here is a stew consisting of such delicate flavors that only the use of spring lamb, the juiciest, most tender lamb available, will do.

2 pounds spring lamb shoulder, cut into 1½-inch cubes
1 stick butter
1 large white onion, sliced thin
2 teaspoons paprika
2 tablespoons tomato paste
3 chicken bouillon cubes, dissolved in 1½ cups boiling water
½ teaspoon black pepper

1 bouquet garni (tie, in a piece of cheesecloth, 1 bay leaf, 2 teaspoons parsley, ¼ teaspoon oregano, and ¼ teaspoon basil)
6 small potatoes, quartered
½ pound fresh mushrooms, cut into thirds and sauteed in butter
1 package frozen green peas
1 cup sour cream

Heat butter in a large pot or a Dutch oven and sauté onion slices until they become soft. Stir in paprika and meat and cook until the lamb is lightly browned on all sides. Stir frequently. Add tomato paste and bouillon, stirring to blend. Add the pepper and drop in the bouquet garni. Bring to a boil. Reduce heat, cover, and simmer one hour. After thirty minutes, add potatoes. After fifty-five minutes remove bouquet garni. Add peas and mushrooms and stir in the sour cream, one spoonful at a time. Heat through and serve immediately.

DUTCH OVEN *(Serves 5 or 6)*

A good deep pot that keeps uniform heat and steams well — that's a Dutch oven. And here is a stew that from start to finish is made in one.

3 slices bacon, diced
2 medium onions, sliced thin
1½ pounds lamb shoulder,
cut into 2-inch cubes
1 teaspoon salt
2 teaspoons paprika
1 can (8 ounces) tomato puree
2 tablespoons fresh parsley, chopped
1 cup sour cream

Sauté diced bacon in a Dutch oven until almost crisp. Add onions and sauté until soft. Add lamb cubes and cook until golden brown on all sides. Stir in salt, paprika, tomato puree, and parsley. Bring to a boil. Reduce the heat, cover, and simmer one and a half hours, adding a little water if needed during cooking. When the meat is tender, stir in the sour cream, one spoonful at a time. Heat through, but do not boil, and serve immediately.

36

MUTTONEER

Mutton may be a little hard to get, but if you insist your butcher will obtain it for you. After trying this delectable stew, you may better understand why the British and Irish like this meat so much.

2 pounds mutton shoulder, cut into 1½-inch cubes
2 teaspoons salt
1 teaspoon black pepper
3 cups water
2 pounds small potatoes, peeled
6 small onions, peeled

Put the mutton into a pot or a Dutch oven and sprinkle with salt and pepper. Stir in the water. Bring to a boil. Reduce heat, cover, and simmer for one hour. Add the potatoes and onions and cook another hour. Add more water, if needed, during the cooking, and serve hot.

LENTILS AND LAMB *(Serves 5)*

Here is another lamb stew, and they are always good. This one introduces lentils into your diet, a delicious seed of a leguminous plant too rarely used in our diets today.

3 medium onions, chopped
3 cloves garlic, minced
¼ teaspoon cayenne pepper
1 teaspoon turmeric
2 teaspoons coriander
1 teaspoon cumin

2 teaspoons salt
2 pounds lamb, cut into 1½-inch cubes
½ cup yogurt
2 cups raw lentils
1 stick butter
4 cups boiling water

Blend together the onions, garlic, cayenne, turmeric, coriander, cumin, and salt. Add the lamb cubes and toss to blend well. Stir in yogurt. Cover and let stand at room temperature for an hour. Meanwhile, put lentils into a pot with enough water to cover. Bring to a boil. Turn off heat and drain. Set to one side.

Melt the butter in a large pot or Dutch oven and pour in the lamb-yogurt mixture. Cook fifteen minutes, stirring frequently to keep from burning. Stir in lentils and boiling water. Cover and simmer half an hour (until meat and lentils are tender). Serve immediately.

FISH AND SEAFOOD STEWS

Among stews made from fresh, off-shore, or deep water animals, it should come as no surprise to learn that oyster is the most popular everywhere in the world.

In fact, oysters raw, oysters fried, oysters stewed, baked, or smoked — everywhere this little mollusk is known — it is revered. And yet, although they have been cultivated for centuries and were farmed in sea beds by the Chinese long before the Christian era, we know little more about them than as objects to be swallowed. They are the least understood of all marine life.

Stop a minute and consider this creature. Is it in fact an aphrodisiac as many believe? Has pollution of our water made them unsafe to eat? What are your chances on opening a shell of finding a pearl? Is the so-called "r" rule true, the one that says they should be eaten only during the months in which the letter "r" occurs?

Let's take a closer look at the oyster and see.

This little bivalve which lost its foot in the course of evolution, and thus its ability to move, nevertheless is one of the few creatures to successfully cross the three barriers that separate all life in the vastness of the aquatic environment — fresh water and salt, warm and cold, deep and shallow — eventually to appear in the off-shore waters of every continent.

It has a mouth, a stomach, two hearts which beat independently, arteries, a highly developed nervous system, and sense and sex organs. Generally a hermaphrodite, it changes sex sometimes annually in an exquisitely refined instinctual drive to maintain a 1:1 ratio in the particular bottom area where it exists.

Its strongest organ is its adductor muscle, the little thing, often dark-colored, by which it is attached to the shell. The adductor muscle is what opens and closes the shell. It also controls the movement of the pleated gill along the oyster's posterior, whose undulations carry food and water to the oyster's mouth (the amount depending on how wide open the valves are) and washes out the waste. Some oysters have been reported to pump as much as thirty-seven quarts of water an hour through themselves in completing this cycle. The adductor muscle is so strong that a force of from twenty-six to thirty-three pounds is needed to tear it apart from the shell.

Men have long believed that consuming oysters, especially raw oysters, would keep them hopping around the bedroom long after others their age have gone to sleep. King Henry the Eighth reputedly ate them daily to help him swing along from wife to wife. Probably it is true that oysters, insofar as any plant or food can sometimes do what love alone can always do, are a stimulant to sex. At least, they certainly are rich in zinc, a mineral which some contemporary medical researchers, investigating what is called the growing impotence of American men, are discovering is a vital element for fertility and male vigor in the sack. Since zinc does not "cook out" in heating (although it is "milled out" in most other foods where it is found), it is believed oysters are a potency factor whether eaten raw or not.

Oysters also contain protein, carbohydrates, glycogen (also called "animal" or "liver starch"), and inorganic constituents such as sodium, potassium, calcium, magnesium, chlorine, bromine, phosphorus, and sulfur.

Contrary to folk belief, oysters may be eaten at any time of the year. The "r" rule might have originated from observations that during the summer months they are watery and contain only a little glycogen. They can be eaten, though, without any danger to health, providing they are kept refrigerated.

Regarding water pollution, oysters contaminated by industrial wastes may show accumulations in large amounts of iron and copper, and some arsenic and lead. Most oysters are purified by chlorination, however, a process used in the United States and Britain. Packers and fish markets generally take the further precaution of washing them again before they are sold.

Digging into your oyster stew, what are your chances of finding a pearl? They are slim, at best, if you live in the United States and consume oysters from Puget Sound and adjacent bays of the East Coast, or what is called Crassostrea virginica. All edible oysters occasionally produce round calcareous concretions; they have no luster and are worthless, so spit them out! True pearls are found only in oysters that inhabit the coral reefs and warm waters of the tropics.

Second to oysters in stew-making from water animals is the chowder king, the clam, the name referring to the tightness with which the shell closes. In its widest usage, clam is a name applied to about fifteen thousand species of bivalve or two-shelled mollusks, including oysters with unequal shells, cockles so dearly loved by the English, scallops, and mussels.

Clams are the forerunners of today's jet-stream form of locomotion over water. Certain Pacific clams, notably the Jackknife, have been observed swimming in rapid spurts by means of water jets expelled about the foot, a powerful muscle with which they can burrow into the bottom of the sea bed and hold so firmly that efforts to dislodge them will frequently break the clam in two.

The most widely used clams for food by Americans are the quahog, ocean quahog, soft shell, and surf clams. All are from the East coast. The best clam in the world is California's geoduck (pronounced gooey-duck). It also is the largest of the Pacific clams, often weighing up to six and a half pounds. It is so delicious and so sought after that in most localities where it is found catches are limited to one clam a day. Small quahogs, also called "cherry stones," are eaten raw. Those and oysters on the half shell are the only animals eaten alive by Americans.

In this chapter you will find the best oyster stew and clam stew recipes ever created. You will also find stews made from crab, shrimp, and lobster, whose flesh so stimulates the stomach glands that it helps to overcome gastric fatigue.

From the world of the bony fish — thirty thousand species at a conservative guess — we have selected two to make stew from that are sure to surprise and delight you. They are the silvery, fresh-water whitefish, and the rugged salmon. Neither are often thought of in connection with stew-making, but both turn out to be excellent dishes.

Many recipes in *The Stew Cookbook* will call for a cream sauce base. This will usually consist of the marriage of butter, flour, and milk or some other liquid.

Please, these sauces require the undivided attention of the cook! We believe in making them over direct heat and therefore they cannot be neglected for a second. If you wish, you may prepare them the old-fashioned way, in a double boiler, but that is much slower. The results simply will turn out better by using the direct heat method.

VIRGINICA *(Serves 4)*

Oyster stew is perhaps the fastest of all stews to prepare, but also one of the most delicate. Care must be taken to see to it that everybody is ready to eat a few minutes after you begin the stew, and greater care must be taken in heating the milk. So follow these directions closely.

1 quart oysters
6 tablespoons butter
½ teaspoon salt
¼ teaspoon black pepper

1 pint milk
1 pint cream (half and half)
½ teaspoon paprika
2 tablespoons parsley, chopped

Drain oysters. Melt four tablespoons of the butter in a large sauce pan and simmer oysters until the edges begin to curl (about three minutes). Stir in salt, pepper, milk, and cream. Heat just to boiling point but do not allow to boil. Ladle into four soup dishes. Sprinkle with paprika and add a dollop of the remaining butter. Add a bit of parsley to each bowl and serve immediately.

(Serves 4) OYSTERS AND PRETZELS

The Dutchmen in Pennsylvania break a few salted pretzels into their oyster stews. It gives a surprising flavor, and the pretzels are much better tasting than those anemic oyster crackers.

1 pint shucked oysters
1 quart milk
1 teaspoon pepper
4 tablespoons butter
4 salted pretzels
Paprika
1 tablespoon parsley, chopped

Put oysters and their liquor into a pan and heat just until the edges curl (about three minutes). Heat milk in another pan just to boiling point (but do not boil). Stir in pepper and combine the oysters and milk. Pour into four bowls. Slip a tablespoon of butter into each bowl. Break a pretzel into each bowl. Sprinkle with paprika and parsley and serve immediately.

FRENCH QUARTER *(Serves 4)*

Here is an oyster-celery stew that's popular in food-loving New Orleans. You will be surprised at how well celery enhances the flavor.

1 pint shucked oysters
4 tablespoons butter
1 can (10½ ounces) cream of celery soup
1 quart milk
½ teaspoon salt
¼ teaspoon pepper
1 teaspoon paprika

Put oysters and their liquor into a pan and heat just until the edges curl (about three minutes). Heat milk and soup in another pan. Allow it to reach boiling point, but do not boil. Stir in salt and pepper and combine the milk and oysters. Heat through and pour into four bowls. Sprinkle with paprika and serve immediately.

Simple to make and delicious to eat, this recipe provides an unusual variation from the usual chowder or steamed clams.

4 cups canned chicken broth
2 cups milk
2 cups cream (half and half)
¼ teaspoon tarragon
1 quart shucked clams, chopped (save the liquor)

Put chicken broth, milk, cream, and tarragon into a sauce pan. Heat through but do not boil. Add the clams and their liquor and cook over very low heat for five minutes. Do NOT let boil. Season to taste and serve hot.

PINCERS *(Serves 4)*

Here is a lobster stew that is quite expensive to make, but we believe you will find it worth every penny. Again, please be careful. With such an expensive ingredient, it would be foolish to allow the milk and cream to curdle. Do not let it boil even a second.

½ pound lobster meat (fresh or canned)
½ pound butter
½ teaspoon black pepper
¼ teaspoon nutmeg
3 cups milk
2 cups cream (half and half)

Cut lobster meat into one-inch cubes. Heat butter in saucepan to sizzling and saute lobster for four minutes, turning frequently to cook all sides. Sprinkle pepper and nutmeg over lobster and stir to blend. Quickly pour milk and cream over lobster, stirring briskly to keep the milk and cream from curdling. Heat to boiling point and serve immediately.

As a variation from the usual broiling, frying, baking, or poaching this always popular fish, here is a recipe — with a haute gastronomie touch — for stewing it.

3 pounds white fish	*1 teaspoon salt*
3 tablespoons butter	*½ teaspoon black pepper*
2 tablespoons olive oil	*1 bay leaf, crumbled*
2 slices bacon, minced	*¼ teaspoon marjoram*
3 tablespoons flour	*¼ teaspoon nutmeg*
1 pint dry white wine	*2 tablespoons parsley, minced*
2 cloves garlic, minced	*¼ cup brandy*

Cut fish into serving size pieces.

Heat butter and oil in large pot or Dutch Oven and sauté bacon until almost crisp. Stir in flour and cook one minute. Gradually stir in the white wine. Add garlic, salt, pepper, bay leaf, marjoram, nutmeg, and parsley. Cover and simmer twenty-five minutes. Add the fish and simmer gently twelve to fifteen minutes, or until fish is tender. Pour into serving bowls.

Heat brandy in a ladle, ignite it, and pour a bit into each bowl.

HERMIT *(Serves 4 to 5)*

Here is another ridiculously easy recipe from those delectable foods from the sea, the crustaceans. Again, do not boil the milk, and also make sure your guests are seated and ready to eat when you start cooking.

3 tablespoons butter
¾ cup fine cracker crumbs
¾ pound crab meat (canned or fresh)
1 quart milk
½ teaspoon salt
¼ teaspoon black pepper
½ cup cream (half and half)
Paprika

Melt butter in stew pan and stir in cracker crumbs and flaked crab meat. Stir in a little of the milk and heat through, stirring lightly to blend. Add salt and pepper, then the remainder of the milk and the cream. Bring just to boiling point and serve immediately, topping each bowl with paprika for color.

GULF OF MEXICO

Here is a little known recipe that is an original with the trawler fishermen in the Gulf who account for the major portion of the world catch of shrimp.

1 pound fresh shrimp, cooked, shelled, and deveined
2 cups milk
2 cups cream (half and half)
3 tablespoons butter
½ teaspoon black pepper
¼ cup dry white wine
2 tablespoons parsley, chopped
Paprika

Put shrimp, milk, cream, butter, and pepper into a sauce pan. Heat to boiling point, but do not boil. Add wine and serve immediately in bowls topped with a bit of parsley and paprika for color.

UPRIVER *(Serves 5 to 6)*

Here is a recipe that produces not only a tasty dish, but one that is fun to eat, too, in discovering the clams in your stew.

12 fresh clams in shell
½ cup olive oil
2 cloves garlic, minced
1 cup onion, chopped fine
1½ cups dry red wine

1 can (16 ounces) tomatoes
1 teaspoon salt
2 tablespoons parsley, minced
½ teaspoon dried red peppers, crushed
1½ pounds fresh salmon, cut into bite-sized pieces

Scrub clams well with a wire brush under cold, running water, and set aside.

Heat oil in sauce pan and sauté garlic and onion until onion is soft. Add the wine and simmer, uncovered, for ten minutes. Drain the tomatoes and add to sauce pan along with the salt, parsley, and red peppers. Stir to blend. Arrange salmon pieces on top of tomatoes. Bring to boil. Reduce heat, cover pan, and simmer fifteen minutes. Arrange clams in a single layer in sauce pan and cook five more minutes with cover on. Discard any clams that do not open. Serve in hot bowls and pass around crusty French or Italian bread slices.

VEGETARIAN STEWS

The creation of a song or a poem to food or drink is not new. Bach wrote a cantata in praise of coffee and Schubert, a trout quintet. Wordsworth's sonnet to wine is well known, and Shelley penned a hymn to plum pudding. But Serge de Diaghilev, the great impresario of the Ballet Russe de Monte Carlo, outdid them all. After reading George Bernard Shaw's essay on vegetarianism he commissioned a ballet to vegetables.

Which is to say that vegetarians are very persuasive people. They have to be: their way of life always has been enlivened by missionary zeal and joking resistance. Like Will Rogers' story of his vegetarian great uncle, who died in the Oklahoma tomato blight of 1869. He was the only human being to do so and the only one who, to his family's embarrassment, had to be embalmed with bicarbonate of soda.

But vegetarianism has an honorable history which it would be wise for flesh eaters to explore. Among other things it has contributed some notable dishes to the fine cuisines of the world — Hungarian Ghivetch and Ratatouille Niçoise from France, for example. Both are stews, by the way.

The first serious advocacy of a fleshless diet began around 500 B.C., more or less simultaneously in India and eastern Mediterranean lands, as part of the philosophical awakening of the time. Pythagoras of Samos is credited with being the first man to articulate the principle that man should not kill needlessly what has feelings and fears death, especially those animals he is most personal with: cats, dogs, horses, garden birds, and house pets. Mystics followed who added the argument that meat-eating was a luxury, gluttonous, cruel, and expensive. And then ascetics came along who, for reasons of abstinence, denied their relish for meat (which is strong flavored: many children do not immediately acquire the taste). They found that a meatless diet gave them little energy to support passions they wanted to suppress, and concluded that men came to act like the animals they ate.

In the modern era, the economic and nutritional schools appeared which advanced the arguments that raising cattle for meat yielded less food per acre than raising, say, protein-rich legumes, and that a fleshless diet is best for human health. The nutritional school notes that most primates are chiefly fruitarians (or frugivores), and that anatomically the human digestive system, with its long intestinal tract, differs in this and other ways from that of such representative carnivores as dogs and cats, in which the lower gut is rather short.

Although the exact effects of particular diets — vegetarian or nonvegetarian — are not yet fully known, out of all this debate one thing has become clear: flesh-eating is not absolutely necessary to health. Simply to drop meat from a typical diet can be dangerous, but only if the meat is not replaced by some other, and equivalent, protein food. And there are equivalents. The old idea that "first class" proteins are found in meat alone has been largely abandoned. The modern demand is for so-called complete proteins, and they are found not only in meat but also in dairy products, soybeans, and nuts.

The vegetarian movement has been carried forward throughout history by ethically inclined individuals such as Shaw and Tolstoi, and by certain religious sects like the Seventh-Day Adventists and the Theosophists. Results have benefitted the world at large. By the early 20th Century, it was contributing substantially to the drive to vary and lighten the nonvegetarian person's diet. Peanut butter and cornflakes both were invented by vegetarians. In India, the railroads have developed a double restaurant system, vegetarian and nonvegetarian.

In sports, vegetarians have won international championships in such fields as running, swimming, tennis, and wrestling. Their records show that vegetarians excel flesh eaters in endurance, but then they, in turn, are excelled in sudden bursts of energy by flesh eaters.

Vegetarians have been prominent in movements opposing cruelty to animals, including inhumane forms of slaughter and laboratory experimentation. They have helped to develop substitutes for fur and leather in clothing. Many join in the contemporary search for agricultural and medical techniques more nearly consistent with natural patterns of organic growth.

But vegetarians do not own the vegetable kingdom, and what a kingdom it is! Think of what a meal without vegetables would be like. Eye and appetite appeal go hand in hand with vegetables at every serving. They are so important to a well-balanced diet that nutritionists have awarded them two places on their chart of the "Seven Basic Food Groups" — green and yellow vegetables in Group 1, and potatoes and other vegetables and fruits in Group 3.

As for vegetable stews, they offer two major advantages over all other stews.

The first is that they can go a long way toward helping us live within our budgets in these days of absurdly exaggerated meat prices, and the meat will scarcely be missed with the stews in this chapter.

The other advantage is one of health. For twenty-five years American housewives have been told to save the water left over from boiling vegetables, to get their full nutriment value. For twenty-five years housewives have tried, but not one in a million actually succeeded. In vegetable stews, that problem is solved without any effort at all — the water comes right along with the stew.

(Serves 4) BARELY BARLEY

This one is a Midwest favorite, and often is available in vegetarian restaurants.

1 can (8 ounces) tomatoes
2 cups water
½ cup carrots, diced
½ cup celery, diced
1 medium onion, diced
1 cup potatoes, peeled and diced
¼ cup barley
2 teaspoons salt
¼ teaspoon black pepper

Put all ingredients into a large pot and bring to a boil. Reduce heat, cover, and simmer for one hour, or until vegetables are tender. Serve hot with hunks of crusty bread spread with butter.

PRESSURE'S ON! *(Serves 6)*

With a pressure cooker everything is possible in just minutes. However, if you do not have one, there is an alternative still making it possible. It just takes a little longer. Read on.

½ head of cabbage, cut up
1 bunch celery, cut up
2 medium onions, diced
1 can (16 ounces) cut green beans, drained
1 can (6 ounces) peas, drained
2 cans (16 ounces each) tomatoes
Salt to taste
2 tablespoons butter

Put everything into a pressure cooker and cook eight minutes.

If you do not have a pressure cooker, put everything into a large kettle and add just enough water to cover. Bring to boil. Reduce heat, cover, and simmer until vegetables are tender. Serve hot.

(Serves 6) CHEESE AND SOY

You will like the cheese and soy sauce touches in this surprisingly easy-to-make dish. For variety, instead of parmesan cheese, you might try other hard cheeses like Pecorino Romano, from ewe's milk, or Caprino Romano, from goat's milk.

11 cups water
1/3 cup soy sauce
2 teaspoons flour
8 carrots, diced
1 can (13 ounces) green beans
1 bay leaf

½ head cabbage
6 medium white potatoes, diced
2 medium onions, diced
1 can (13 ounces) corn
Salt and pepper to taste
½ cup parmesan cheese, grated

Pour ten cups of water into a large Dutch oven. Mix soy sauce with the flour and one cup of water. Stir into Dutch oven. Bring pot to boil and add carrots, green beans, and bay leaf. Reduce heat, cover, and simmer thirty minutes. After thirty minutes, remove bay leaf and add the cabbage, potatoes, onions, and corn. Simmer thirty more minutes, being careful that nothing sticks during the cooking. Add a little more water if necessary. Season to taste with salt and pepper and just before serving sprinkle the cheese over top of stew.

LITTLE ITALY *(Serves 6)*

Italy has the smallest per capita number of vegetarians than any other Western European country. It's a fact to ponder. Still, one of them made up this stew using all of his favorite foods except meat and pasta, and we thank him.

1 zucchini (1 pound), diced
1 small eggplant, pared and diced
1 medium onion, diced
2 large green peppers, diced
3 medium tomatoes, peeled and diced
6 cans (6 ounces each) tomato paste

½ teaspoon allspice
3 bay leaves
Salt to taste
¼ pound parmesan cheese,
  cut into tiny cubes

Place all ingredients except cheese into a large kettle. Add enough water to cover. Bring to boil, stirring constantly. Reduce heat, cover, and simmer fifteen to twenty minutes, or until vegetables are crisply tender. Stir in cubed cheese and serve immediately.

(Serves 4) ON THE BUTTON

This is truly a mushroom stew, and a quite unusual one, being fully balanced by the addition of nuts, which contain the most concentrated form of protein there is.

2 cans (14 ounces each) cut green beans, plus liquid
1 jar (8 ounces) button mushrooms
¼ cup onion, minced
1 cup chopped walnuts

Mix all ingredients in a large casserole. Cover and place in a preheated 350-degree oven. Bake fifty minutes. Let cool five minutes before serving so you do not burn your tongue on the piping hot nuts.

WEEKENDER *(Serves 6)*

A good deep skillet is all that is needed for the Weekender Stew, which makes a dish that is special enough to serve for Sunday dinner.

6 carrots, sliced
6 potatoes, diced
8 small whole onions
2 medium green peppers, quartered
2 tablespoons cooking oil
1 medium onion, chopped
1 cup celery, chopped
2 cloves garlic, minced

1 can (16 ounces) tomatoes
1 cup water
½ teaspoon black pepper
1 bay leaf, crumbled
1/8 teaspoon basil
1/8 teaspoon marjoram
1 teaspoon fresh parsley, chopped
Salt to taste

Sauté carrots, potatoes, onions, and peppers in a skillet with cooking oil until lightly browned (about fifteen minutes). Remove vegetables from skillet with slotted spoon.

Sauté chopped onion, celery, and garlic until onion is translucent. Add tomatoes, water, pepper, bay leaf, basil, and marjoram. Stir vegetables back into skillet. Cover and simmer until tender crisp (ten to twelve minutes). Be careful not to cook until mixture is mushy. Add salt and parsley and serve.

(Serves 4) BED OF RICE

Rice, especially and often exclusively brown rice, is a vegetarian staple food. This stew perfectly complements a dish of rice and raises it from ordinary fare to almost gourmet status.

2 medium onions, sliced thin
1 medium green pepper, minced
3 tablespoons cooking oil
1 tablespoon paprika
¼ teaspoon salt
1 pound fresh mushrooms, washed
in cold water and cut into thirds

Sauté onions and green pepper in cooking oil until onions are soft. Stir in paprika and salt. Add mushrooms and just enough water to cover. Bring to a boil. Reduce heat, cover, and simmer for fifteen minutes. Stir occasionally to keep from sticking. Serve hot over a bed of rice.

A BIT CORNY *(Serves 6)*

The unusual is what stew is all about, and here is one you are not likely soon to forget. It's from Illinois, by the way.

6 ribs celery, cliced in 1-inch pieces
8 carrots, peeled and sliced into 1-inch pieces
2 medium onions, sliced
1 can (8 ounces) peas
1 can (13 ounces) corn
4 medium potatoes, peeled and diced

1 can (16 ounces) tomatoes
2 teaspoons salt
1 tablespoon sugar
2 tablespoons tapioca
1 cup tomato juice
1 tablespoon dry sherry

Arrange celery, carrots, onions, peas, corn, potatoes, and tomatoes (in that order) in layers in a casserole. Add juice from the canned vegetables. Sprinkle over the top the salt, sugar, tapioca, tomato juice, and sherry. Cover and bake in preheated 250-degree oven for four hours. Serve hot.

(Serves 6) GREEN PEPPER

Looks are deceiving. Although a simple appearing dish, this is a most unusual stew, very easily prepared, and among the most palatable of vegetarian stews.

2 medium onions, chopped
3 tablespoons butter
5 medium green peppers, chopped
2 cans (16 ounces each) tomatoes and juice
1 teaspoon celery salt
½ teaspoon garlic salt

½ cup water
3 medium potatoes, diced and precooked 5 minutes in boiling water
1 teaspoon salt
½ teaspoon black pepper

Sauté onions in butter until soft. Add green pepper and tomatoes. Add celery salt and garlic salt and water. Cover and simmer forty-five minutes. Add potatoes and continue simmering until potatoes are tender. Stir in salt and pepper and serve.

IT'S A DILLY *(Serves 6)*

There's always a place for the Old World's aromatic herb dill, and it's not exclusively in a pickled cucumber, either. How about in a kind of packaged vegetarian stew, for example?

4 cups water
1 teaspoon salt
¼ teaspoon dill weed
1 medium green pepper, chopped
1 teaspoon parsley, chopped
1 package (1¾ ounce) vegetable soup mix

1 tablespoon instant minced onion
2 cups carrots, sliced
2 cups celery, sliced
2 cups potatoes, peeled and cut up
1 can (10½ ounces)
  cream of celery soup

Place all ingredients, except soup, into large kettle. Cover and simmer on top of stove until ingredients are just tender (about 20 minutes). Stir in cream of celery soup, heat through, stirring to blend, and serve.

(Serves 4) PAPPY'S PAPRIKA

Caraway seeds and a generous portion of paprika feature another delicious vegetarian stew from the Midwest.

2 medium onions, sliced thin
1 medium green pepper, minced
3 tablespoons cooking oil
1 tablespoon paprika
1 teaspoon salt
1 pound potatoes, peeled and cubed

1 pound carrots, scraped and cut crosswise into 1-inch pieces
1 tablespoon caraway seeds
3 tablespoons ketchup
Water to cover

Sauté onions and green pepper in cooking oil until onions are soft. Stir in paprika and salt. Add potatoes, carrots, caraway seeds, and ketchup, and add water just to cover. Bring to boil. Reduce heat, cover, and simmer until potatoes and carrots are tender (about twenty minutes). Add a bit more water from time to time if necessary, and stir frequently to keep from sticking. Serve hot.

SAUCY *(Serves 4 to 5)*

The last vegetarian stew is done with a white sauce, which makes it rather like a "stew fricassee."

1 cup carrots, diced
1 cup celery, diced
1 cup cabbage, cut up
1 cup green beans, sliced
1 cup potatoes, diced
1 medium onion, chopped
2 teaspoons parsley, chopped

2 tablespoons bread crumbs
2 tablespoons butter

Sauce ingredients
1½ tablespoons butter
2 tablespoons flour
2 cups milk

Place carrots, celery, cabbage, and green beans in a pot with water to cover and cook eight minutes. Add potatoes and onion and place in a casserole.

Make sauce by melting the one and a half tablespoons butter in a sauce pan. Stir in flour and cook two minutes, stirring to keep from burning. Gradually add the milk and cook gently until it begins to thicken. Pour over vegetables in casserole and stir in. Sprinkle with parsley and bread crumbs and dot with the two tablespoons of butter. Bake in a preheated 350-degree oven fifteen minutes and serve.

COMMON'ST
CREATURE STEWS

Grandmother of 1945 would be surprised at how far the lowly chicken has come in the geologic time scale minute or two since the end of World War II.

It used to be, and forty centuries of tradition had held it so, that she was required to "dress" a chicken before cooking it and setting it out for the family to eat. That was quite a job. Often it included wringing the creature's neck and tearing out its feathers — being careful to pluck the pesky pin feathers with the point of a knife. Then she would singe the bird over an open flame to remove what bits of feather she had missed. Only after all that did she proceed to the tricky job of removing the innards and cleaning it thoroughly before she tossed it into the stew pot, oven, or skillet.

Today it's a whole new ball game with the commonest creature in man's food kingdom. Commercial hatcheries, electronic computers, intensive feeding systems, and specially built plants produce stunned, bled, defeathered, eviscerated, frozen, and even wrapped, jointed, and cooked chicken by assembly line methods. Five great poultry markets have emerged — Chicago, New York, Philadelphia, Boston, and San Francisco — which distribute almost a billion chickens a year to the nation's tables. Breeding has become so sophisticated that a good chicken farmer can raise in the same battery-operated brooder stock with different skin color to suit his market — usually white for the English and yellow for the United States and much of continental Europe.

In the matter of breeding, alone, so many refinements have been made with this creature that it wouldn't surprise poultry lovers one day to find that somebody had crossed a chicken and a turkey and got a chickey or a turkhen.

Does that sound foolish? Well, Charles Darwin thought it could be done. Among his papers on evolution is one in which he states that all domestic fowl are cross-breedable because all have sprung from a single species, the wild jungle fowl still found in a wild state in India and called *gallus bankiva.*

He based his belief on the fact that *gallus bankiva* closely resembled the Black Breasted Red

Game Hen of today, one of the oldest varieties of domestic fowl known; that the Black Breasted Red crosses readily with the common hen, producing fertile offspring; that it resembles the domestic fowl in voice and action, and that it crosses equally well with other wild species as it does with the hen.

The question as to whether chickens and turkeys can be crossbred has intrigued poultry farmers for at least a century, but very little has been done about proving it. The advantages of such a mating are obvious: turkeys do not boil nor do they fry well (although some fryer-roasters produced from Beltsville Small Whites are gaining in popularity). Turkeys have the reputation of beging extremely troublesome to raise, and there is much folklore surrounding feeding methods that are thought to be successful. Crossing them, then, might produce a stewing turkey, easier to rear, and could allow the industry to break out of its festival day syndrome and into the general market.

One interesting attempt to mate turkeys and chickens has been made, though, but not in the United States. It occurred in Sumatra, the land of bats, flying squirrels, tree shrews, flying lemurs, wild dogs and boars, the civet cat, and many beautiful butterflies, where competitive showing of decorative poultry is a national pastime.

It happened in 1967 when a Batak millionaire named Tri Som Dingh imported some young toms and stag turkeys from the U.S. Dingh already owned the three-time Indonesia national champion rooster, and birds of every feather flew around his thousand-acre farm just outside of Padang. As a breeder, his fame was Asia-wide. He owned domestic fowl with plumage laced, penciled, striped, barred, and also solid-colored stock including red, buff, black, white, and blue. Many of his fowls had eyes varying in color from black to pearl, bay, or gray; fowls with rose combs, single or pea combs, leaf combs, spike combs; fowls with or without beards and crests and showing in their feathers every color of the spectrum.

But the results of Dingh's noble experiment were doomed from the start for a curious reason: no mating occurred because the temperatures of the Malay Archipelago drained the American cobblers of their energy. The hot and extremely moist air also induced respiratory infections in them, which immediately affected their sinuses, and they all died of pneumonia.

But getting back to Grandmother. She also believed firmly in the folk saying among chicken farmers that when an old hen's body sags, her eyes dim, her disposition sours, her comb dries down, her wattles and earlobes grow small and limp, and her pelvic arches stiffen, she is ripe to be stewed. It is then that she passes into another state, one which might be called a state of Grace. Her meat is fat and tough enough to boil for hours, and she has become prized for the richness of her fatty flavor. According to that folk belief, all soups and stews must be made from old hens.

That no longer is true, thanks to hybrids developed since World War II. Any kind of chicken can be used for stews today. True, there are roasters, broilers, fryers, poussin, and capons, all providing their special tastes. But beyond that, each in cooking is versatile to the widest extreme. Young, tender birds nowadays take as well to moist heat as do older ones, with the additional benefits that they are cheaper and do not take so long to cook. Besides, try to find an old hen anymore at your supermarket. You might get one, by special order, but the normal supply of them is cornered by the makers of soups and bouillons.

Therefore, for all the recipes in this chapter except the one that specifically calls for a stewing chicken, just pick up the package of chicken of your choice, and proceed with confidence that you are going to make a splendid stew.

There is much more to say about man's fine feathered friend, the chicken.

It is by far the oldest of our domesticated animals, with the earliest records of them found in a Chinese encyclopedia compiled almost four thousand years ago. They were mentioned by Aristophanes in his comedies, and they figure on Babylonian pottery. Aristotle, Plutarch, Aeschylus, Plato, and Pliny all wrote about them, and the slogan "a chicken in every pot" was a campaign cry in the first general election ever held in Rome. They were imported into the British Isles by the Romans, who regarded them as sacred to Mars. The bantam rooster has been exalted in all ages as an emblem symbolizing bravery in defense, and the French used the cock on their ensign after the Revolution. The cock also figures in the Bible and has often been used in Christian art to symbolize the Resurrection. At the present time it is regarded by political parties all over the world as a herald to victory and to a new day that never seems to come. But that isn't the cock's fault.

But all that belongs in another book. Now, on to chicken stews!

HAM IT UP *(Serves 4 to 5)*

Pieces of ham and the pervasive influence of a dried red pepper make this a most unusual chicken stew.

1 tablespoon butter
1 tablespoon flour
1 large white onion, thinly sliced
1 chicken (about 3 pounds)
  cut into serving pieces
½ pound boiled ham, chopped
1 small dried red pepper

1 teaspoon thyme
2 teaspoons parsley, chopped
1 can (16 ounces) tomatoes
1 rib celery, chopped
½ teaspoon paprika
1 quart water

Get butter sizzling in a large pot. Stir in the flour and blend well. Add onion slices and chicken pieces and cook and stir until chicken is browned lightly on all sides. Add all other ingredients. Bring to boil. Reduce heat, cover, and simmer one hour. Serve hot with fluffy rice.

RIGHT ON THYME

A bit complicated in preparation, but if you are especially fond of the white meat of chicken, this one is for you.

2 chicken breasts	*½ cup flour*
1 rib celery, cut up	*¼ teaspoon thyme*
1 teaspoon salt	*1 teaspoon salt*
2 cups chicken broth	*¼ teaspoon black pepper*
½ pound tiny white onions	*1 teaspoon Worcestershire sauce*
6 medium-sized carrots, cut in 3-inch pieces	*1 can (8 ounces) lima beans*
1 stick butter	

Place chicken breasts, celery and salt in pot with water to cover. Bring to boil. Reduce heat, cover, and simmer twenty minutes (until chicken is tender). Let cool, then skin and debone chicken breasts and cut into large pieces. Set to one side. Strain and save two cups chicken broth.

Put chicken broth, onions, and carrots into large pot and bring to a boil. Reduce heat, cover, and simmer until vegetables are tender (about twelve minutes).

Get butter sizzling hot in a saucepan. Stir in the flour, blending well. Cook two minutes, stirring to keep from burning. Stir in thyme, salt, pepper, and Worcestershire sauce. Pour chicken broth into flour mixture slowly, stirring constantly. Add lima beans and simmer until sauce begins to thicken. Add chicken pieces and carrots and onions. Heat through and serve immediately.

PRETTY NUTTY *(Serves 6)*

Peanuts have a difficult time of it getting themselves into recipes — maybe because they're so much fun just to eat out of hand. Here is one they're in, and the taste surprise they provide is a delight.

1 cut-up chicken (3 pounds)
1½ cups water
1 can (16 ounces) tomatoes
1 medium onion, chopped
2 bay leaves, crumbled
2 cloves garlic, minced
½ teaspoon salt
1 teaspoon oregano

2 teaspoons lemon juice
½ teaspoon chili powder
1 can (10 ounces) ripe olives
½ cup peanuts, crushed fine
1 cup dry sherry
2 teaspoons cornstarch, dissolved in a bit of cold water

Put chicken, water, tomatoes, onion, bay leaves, garlic, salt, oregano, and lemon juice in a pot. Bring to boil. Reduce heat, cover, and simmer fifteen minutes. Stir in chili powder. Chop olives and stir in along with the peanuts and sherry. Cover and simmer thirty more minutes. Stir in cornstarch-water mixture and simmer and stir until stew begins to thicken. Serve hot with fluffy whipped potatoes.

A ROSY GLOW

Peppers and the Tabasco sauce made from their fruit are nature's hot little coals. So stoke up your fire and bask in this one.

1 cut-up chicken (3 pounds)
2 teaspoons salt
2 teaspoons paprika
½ stick butter
2 medium onions, sliced
1 large green pepper, chopped
3 cups water
1 can (16 ounces) tomatoes and juice

3 tablespoons parsley, chopped
½ teaspoon Tabasco sauce
2 teaspoons Worcestershire sauce
2 cans (8 ounces each) Mexican-style kernel corn
1 tablespoon cornstarch, dissolved in a bit of cold water

Sprinkle chicken on all sides with salt and paprika. Heat butter to sizzling in large pot and sauté chicken pieces until they are golden brown on all sides. Add onions and green pepper and saute until the onions are soft. Add water, tomatoes, parsley, Tabasco and Worcestershire sauce. Bring to a boil. Reduce heat, cover, and simmer fifteen minutes. Add the corn and simmer, covered, thirty more minutes (until chicken is tender). Stir in cornstarch-water mixture and simmer and stir until stew thickens. Serve hot.

A WING AND A PRAYER (Serves 4)

Don't be afraid to use your fingers on this dish, to make certain none of the delicious morsels of chicken get away from you.

2 pounds chicken wings
2 teaspoons salt
1 tablespoon flour
2 teaspoons paprika
4 tablespoons butter
1 large onion, chopped
1 rib celery, chopped
2 cloves garlic, chopped

1 teaspoon thyme
½ teaspoon basil
1 teaspoon pepper
2 chicken bouillon cubes
1 cup dry sherry (or water)
1 tablespoon cornstarch, dissolved in a bit of cold water

Sprinkle chicken wings with salt, flour, and paprika. Get butter sizzling hot in a large pot and sauté wings for five minutes, stirring often to keep them from sticking. Add onion, celery, and garlic and sauté until onion is soft. Add thyme, basil, pepper, bouillon cubes, and sherry. Scrape bottom of the pan with a spatula. Bring to a boil. Reduce heat, cover, and simmer for forty-five minutes. Stir in cornstarch-water mixture and continue simmering and stirring until it thickens. Serve hot with rice.

BRUNSWICK

The South's claim to fame in the stew world is this old standby, which has been popular there for more than two hundred years.

1 cut-up chicken (3 pounds)
4 cups water
6 slices bacon, diced
¼ teaspoon crushed red pepper
4 potatoes, sliced thin
1 medium onion, chopped

1 package (12 ounces) frozen lima beans
1 package (12 ounces) frozen kernel corn
4 tomatoes, cut into quarters
1 teaspoon salt
1 teaspoon black pepper
¼ teaspoon marjoram

Put chicken and water into a large kettle. Add diced bacon and crushed red pepper. Bring to a boil. Reduce heat, cover, and simmer forty minutes (until chicken is tender). Add potato slices, onion, and lima beans. Simmer until potatoes are tender. Add corn, tomatoes, salt, black pepper and marjoram, and simmer another ten minutes, and serve.

GRANNY'S DUMPLINGS *(Serves 5 to 6)*

Chicken and dumplings and gravy, here is the most popular of all chicken stews. And for this one nothing but a fat old hen will do, because of the rich gravy it will make.

1 stewing chicken (4 or 5 pounds)
1 large onion, chopped
2 teaspoons salt
1 teaspoon pepper
2 carrots, scraped and cut into chunks
4 ribs celery, cut into 3-inch pieces
Water to cover

Into a large pot place chicken, onion, salt, pepper, carrots, celery, and enough water to just cover. Bring to boil. Reduce heat, cover, and simmer two and a half hours, until chicken is tender.

(continued) # GRANNY'S DUMPLINGS

Dumplings

1 cup water
½ stick butter
½ teaspoon salt
1 cup sifted flour
1 egg, lightly beaten

Mix dumpling batter by putting water on to boil in a pot. Add butter and salt and remove from heat when butter is melted. Stir in flour and mix thoroughly. Add the egg and stir briskly. Drop batter, a tablespoonful at a time, into hot chicken broth and simmer (do not let boil) for five minutes. Serve chicken and dumplings immediately.

FRISKY FRICASSEE *(Serves 4)*

America's favorite way to stew a chicken is for fricassee. Here is a superb recipe that will call for encores every time!

1 teaspoon salt
¼ teaspoon pepper
¾ cup flour
2 whole chicken breasts, skinned
and chopped into quarters
4 tablespoons butter

½ small onion, peeled
2 ribs celery, chopped
1 bay leaf
2 cups canned chicken broth
2 teaspoons cornstarch, dissolved
in a bit of cold water

Combine salt, pepper, and flour. Dredge chicken pieces in flour to coat well.

Brown chicken pieces in butter over moderate heat in a large skillet. Add onion, celery, bay leaf, and chicken broth. Cover and simmer thirty minutes.

Remove onion, celery, and bay leaf and discard. Remove chicken pieces to serving platter to keep warm. Stir cornstarch-water mixture into broth and cook until sauce thickens, using a little more cornstarch and water if necessary. Pour sauce over chicken and serve hot with noodles, dumplings, or whipped potatoes.

GOURMET STEWS

When it comes to the word "gourmet" a great many people throw up their hands, look defensive, and say, "Who me? That's too ritzy. Just pass the Mulligan Stew, won'tcha, please?"

What scares these people is not the prospect of fine food and hearty eating. They merely are intimidated by the endless flap thrown out by the pseudo-gourmet, about *his* tastes, *his* favorite dishes, *his* rosy-lipped gourmandise. If the truth were known probably more hogs and gluttons would be found per capita among this phony crowd than among plain meat and potatoes people.

So don't be scared away by this chapter title. Treats are in store for you that you haven't begun to imagine. Withstand the bluff and buffoonery of the pseudo-gourmet and see for yourself what the excitement over fine food is all about.

To begin with, the true gourmet attitude is not a ritzy one at all nor does it exclude mother cooking for the family. It manifests itself in a robust love of food and a sure instinct for knowing how to prepare or where to get what is good. A true gourmet may be well-traveled or, like Thoreau, live alone in the woods. He can even be the premiere clown of the Shrine Circus, like Joe Sherman, who says, "There are no clowns. Nobody is going into clowning anymore. But cooking? Well, that's something else again." What distinguishes a gourmet cook like Joe Sherman from slobs is his attention to detail and his keen enjoyment in making or eating a dish carefully prepared. It doesn't matter whether that dish is exotic, a sturdy one like stew, or one made out of Thoreau's shrubs, herbs, and seeds.

In cooking, invention is not the gourmet's chief talent. Patience counts more. One can imagine the hours great chefs like Escoffier or Sti Beauchard used to stand over their pots of boiling bones, skimming off the froth, until those bones had released the last vestige of their gelatin and marrow to base the perfect stock. Few gourmet favorites have been created by gourmets. Most often, like the French Pot-au-Feu and Bouillabaisse stews, or the Spanish Paella, they originated in the countryside and were brought to the tables of the rich by farmers or servants. Gourmet, by the way, comes from the old French word *gromet*, which meant wine merchant's servant, influenced in a sense by the Middle English *gourmand,* or glutton.

As a term of honor the label gourmet belongs strictly to modern times. There were no gourmets in ancient Rome. People then considered themselves savage eaters. Dining was held by the wellborn to be something done only in the privacy of the home or in a banquet hall filled with men only. The idea of ingesting through a hole in the face particles of food that others could see floating through the cavern of the mouth, was too repellent for the refined natures of the time to contemplate. Only one's children or wife or closest friends were permitted to witness so base an act of eating.

To be sure, there were *tabernae meritoria* (better class taverns) to dine in, but these were held in such contempt that men veiled themselves before entering. Eggs, goose liver pate, ham, cheese, fowl, and game were displayed in front to draw customers. But once inside the fare was more likely to be soup, twice-boiled cabbage, or boiled sheep's head, all highly seasoned with garlic, onions, and pungent sauce, the commonest base for which was the juice from putrid fish entrails.

Pseudo-gourmets wax militant on the subject of women. "Women just cannot be gourmets," they say. Yet history's first gourmet was a woman, Catherine de Medicis, the Italian-born queen of France in the sixteenth century. Early in the reign of her husband, Henry II, with the help of cooks imported from Italy, she began to revolutionize cookery in Paris. Her ideas spread through hungry France like dye. By 1765 when A. Boulanger, a soup vendor, opened the world's first "restaurant," or "restorative," Frenchmen had become discriminating and nobles vied with each other over the excellence of their cooks. To have been a son or grandson of somebody who worked in a Medicis kitchen (and there were many, for she fired her kitchen help as cavalierly as she ordered the Massacre of St. Bartholomew), was like once having worked at Cafe Maxim de Paris today.

Gourmandise as we know it took its great leap forward after the French Revolution. So many nobles had their heads chopped off, leaving so many jobless cooks, that to survive many of those cooks opened eating houses. By 1804 Paris had from five to six hundred restaurants, and to dine in them had become the fashion. Similarly, to know which one to dine in for which particular dish had become known as gourmandise.

French cuisine from Catherine de Medicis forward has generally been agreed upon to be the luxury cuisine of the world. In some great cities, Rio de Janeiro, for example, it is the only fare served at the better hotels and restaurants. It is almost impossible to find bad food in any of the present three thousand restaurants in Paris, so it is a gourmet's paradise. Imagine, if one went from restaurant to restaurant sampling one dish a day, with each restaurant featuring seven dishes on its menu (the average for the smaller Paris cafes), it would take a conscientious gourmet almost sixty years to cover them all. Is it any wonder that appreciation is more important to a gourmet than invention?

So that is the way it is with gourmandise. Knowing where and what is as important as knowing how. Regarding gourmet stews, this is where *The Stew Cookbook* comes in. We will show you the where and what in gourmet stews, and also the how, making you a triple-threat in a restaurant, in the kitchen, or at your own table.

In this chapter you will find stews that are far above the average. All are easily made if you pay attention, and all, once prepared, will be greedily devoured by your family and friends. These stews include the Spanish Cocido and Paella; Pot-au-Feu, Bouillabaisse and the wonderful Cassolet of Paris; the famous Carbonnades a la Flamande of Belgium; Mulligatawny from India, and the Jambalaya from our own South.

A word about Paella (liberally translated, Paella means "ears"). Traditionally it is served at table directly from the pan it is cooked in. In Spain, this is a shallow iron skillet with handles (or ears) on each side. It is not likely that the average American household will have one of these utensils so a normal skillet will do just as well.

The Spanish never stir a Paella once the rice is added, nor do they cover the skillet while cooking. We have found, however, that if you partly cover the skillet during the last few minutes of cooking, the rice will gain moisture and therefore be more tasty.

The golden glow usually associated with Paella is achieved with the addition of saffron to the rice. Now, saffron surely is the world's most expensive spice. But so little of it is used in Paella that it is well worth the expense.

Cocido features chick peas which are called garbanzos. These are square-shaped, light brown beans and can be purchased raw, soaked overnight, and cooked. They also can be purchased in cans, already cooked, and for the purpose of the recipes in *The Stew Cookbook* that is the variety we prefer.

If you are serving a green salad with your Cocido, sprinkle a few garbanzos into it. They are delightful.

QUIXOTE *(Serves 4 or 5)*

Here is a version of Paella we enjoyed on the beach in a restaurant just outside crowded Torremolinos. The restaurant owner swore the recipe was used to feed the Man of La Mancha's large family.

2 tablespoons flour
½ teaspoon salt
2 chicken breasts, skinned, deboned, and cut into pieces
½ cup olive oil
1½ pounds raw shrimp, shelled and deveined
1 chorizo (or other garlic sausage) sliced
1 medium-sized onion, chopped

3 garlic cloves, chopped fine
2 firm tomatoes, peeled and chopped
1 can (3½ ounces) pimento strips
1 can (7½ ounces) minced clams
½ teaspoon saffron
2 cups raw (not instant) rice
1 package frozen peas
1 quart canned chicken broth

Sprinkle the flour and salt over chicken pieces. Get olive oil hot in a Paella pan (or any big skillet) and cook chicken until the pieces are golden brown. Remove chicken to another pan and save. Place shrimp and sliced sausage into skillet and cook three minutes, stirring frequently. Add shrimp and sausage to chicken.

Place onion, garlic, and tomatoes into skillet and cook until onion is soft (add a little oil if necessary). Return chicken, shrimp, and sausage to skillet and add the pimento strips. Add minced clams and their juice. Stir in rice and saffron, blending well. Stir in peas. Get chicken broth boiling and pour over everything in the skillet. Place, uncovered, in a 300-degree oven for ten to fifteen minutes (most of the moisture should be absorbed by then). Serve immediately from skillet.

(Serves 6) ROYAL PAELLA

Here is another paella which is a little easier to prepare. Easy or not, it is a true gourmet feast often found in better restaurants along the Costa del Sol.

2 chicken breasts
2 lobster tails
½ pound sausage (Italian, Polish, or Spanish)
½ pound boiled ham
2 large tomatoes
1 package frozen peas
½ cup olive oil
1 pound uncooked shrimp

2 cups long grain rice
¼ teaspoon garlic powder
¼ teaspoon saffron
2 teaspoons paprika
1½ teaspoons salt
1 teaspoon black pepper
4½ cups boiling water

Cut chicken and lobster tails, unboned, into two-inch pieces. Slice ham into thin strips and cut sausages into two-inch pieces. Chop tomatoes.

Get oil hot in paella pan or skillet. Lightly brown chicken pieces. Remove to another pan. Shell shrimp and cook in same oil for one and one half minutes. Add to chicken pieces.

Put rice into oil and cook two minutes, stirring to keep from sticking. Combine all other ingredients with rice. Pour in boiling water and cook uncovered, on top of stove over high heat, for ten minutes. Reduce heat and simmer ten more minutes, or until most of liquid is absorbed and rice is tender. Serve immediately.

EL PUEBLO COCIDO *(Serves 6)*

Cocido is probably the national stew of Spain. It is cooked and served in all parts of the country, but is especially popular in the north and in Madrid. Here is a typical Cocido.

*2 pounds breast of veal,
  cut into 2-inch cubes
¼ cup olive oil
4 medium-sized onions, sliced
3 cloves garlic, minced
2 firm tomatoes, cut into quarters
½ cup fresh parsley, chopped
½ pound boiled ham, chopped*

*1 ham bone
6 chicken wings
8 cups water
1 teaspoon salt
2 cans (20 ounces each) chick peas
(or garbanzos)
1 package frozen carrots, cubed*

Brown meat in a large sauce pan or Dutch oven in the olive oil. Add onions, garlic, tomatoes, parsley, ham, ham bone, chicken wings, water, and salt. Bring to boil and stir to blend well. Reduce heat, cover, and simmer three and a half to four hours (until meat is tender). Add more water during cooking if necessary. Stir in chick peas and carrots. Simmer five more minutes and serve hot. If you wish a thicker stew, mix one tablespoon of cornstarch with a bit of cold water, stir it into stew, and simmer until it thickens.

(Serves 6 to 8) BARDOT

The movie stars and jet setters who sun themselves in the south of France love this version of Bouillabaisse which is served, with variations depending on the fish catch of the day, in almost every restaurant along the French Riviera.

1 pound raw shrimp, shelled and deveined
2 teaspoons salt
2 cloves garlic, chopped
2 tablespoons parsley, chopped
1 small bay leaf, crumbled
½ teaspoon thyme
¼ teaspoon saffron
½ teaspoon black pepper
½ cup dry white wine

2 pounds any fresh white fish
1 pound fresh sea bass
2 lobster tails
2 dozen mussels in shells
¼ cup olive oil
1 leek, chopped
1 large onion, chopped
1 carrot, chopped
2 ribs celery, chopped fine
2 large tomatoes, chopped

Have white fish and bass cleaned but not boned. Cut crosswise into two-inch pieces. Also cut lobster tails crosswise (shell and all) into three-inch pieces. Scrub mussels well under cold running water. Set all the seafood aside.

Get oil hot in a large kettle and sauté leek, onion, carrot, and celery until onion is soft. Add tomatoes, shrimp, salt, garlic, parsley, bay leaf, thyme, saffron, black pepper, and wine and simmer ten minutes. Arrange the seafood attractively on top of vegetables. Add just enough water to cover all. Bring to a boil. Reduce heat and simmer, covered, for fifteen minutes. Divide mixture into large bowls and serve hot with hunks of French bread.

PRETTY PORKY *(Serves 4)*

A pork and bean dish that is truly different is the Cassolet stew from provincial France. It can be made with lamb, too. In fact, it is made in hundreds of ways, but the one ingredient it always contains is beans.

1½ pounds boneless pork
3 tablespoons lard
1 garlic sausage, sliced
½ pound salt pork, cut into
½-inch cubes
1 pig's foot, scrubbed under
cold, running water
2 cans (8 ounces each) beef broth
1 tablespoon tomato paste

½ pound dried white beans,
soaked overnight
1 large onion, peeled and stuck
with 2 cloves
1 bay leaf, ½ teaspoon thyme, and
2 tablespoons parsley tied in a
piece of cheesecloth
2 teaspoons salt
1 teaspoon black pepper

Cut pork into two and one half inch cubes. Get lard hot in a large kettle and brown pork pieces on all sides. Add the sausage, salt pork, and pig's foot. Simmer gently, covered, for twenty minutes. Add beef broth and simmer covered, for one hour. Meanwhile, cook the beans with the onion, the spice bag, salt and pepper in enough water to cover for thirty minutes. Add beans, along with the tomato paste, to the meats and simmer gently, covered, one more hour. Discard the spice bag, check the seasoning, and serve hot with hunks of French bread.

(Serves 6) POT ON THE FIRE

As beef stew is America's favorite, so is Pot-Au-Feu to France. It's a dish to serve for six hungry persons, and is not for picky eaters.

3 pounds boneless beef
½ pound salt pork, cut into ½-inch cubes
1 large onion, stuck with 2 whole cloves
4 leeks, cut into 3-inch pieces
1 medium-sized turnip, quartered
2 teaspoons chopped parsley
1 teaspoon thyme

2 teaspoons salt
1 stewing chicken, cut into serving pieces
6 carrots, scraped and cut into 2-inch pieces
6 potatoes, peeled
1 small head cabbage, quartered

Put the beef, salt pork, onion, leeks, turnip, parsley, thyme, and salt into a large pot. Add enough water to cover. Bring to a boil and, using a slotted spoon, skim froth from top of water. Reduce heat, cover, and simmer one and a half hours. Add the cut-up chicken and simmer thirty minutes. Add the carrots, potatoes, and cabbage and continue cooking, covered, for another thirty minutes (Everything now should be tender.) Slice the meat and divide everything equally in large bowls. Remove onion with cloves before serving. Serve hot with hunks of French bread.

HOT AND RICH *(Serves 6)*

A tantalizing stew that we have been serving at parties successfully for years utilizes a stewing chicken stuffed with chili powder sprinkled on bacon slices. The flavor is unforgettable.

4 slices thick bacon
1 tablespoon chili powder
2 teaspoons garlic salt
1 stewing chicken (4 to 5 pounds)
2 tablespoons butter
2 large onions, chopped
2 cloves garlic, minced
1 green pepper, chopped

1 cup tomato puree
3 tablespoons chili powder
½ cup Madeira wine
2 tablespoons cornstarch, dissolved in a bit of cold water
¼ cup sliced almonds, toasted in a bit of butter
1 pound mushroom caps, sauteed in butter

Cut bacon in half and spread with chili powder and garlic salt. Roll each slice and tuck into chicken cavity. Skewer end of chicken. Put in a large pot breast down. Melt butter and sauté onion, garlic and green pepper until soft. Add tomato puree, the three tablespoons of chili powder, and wine. When mixture boils, pour over chicken. Add boiling water to cover three-fourths. Cover and simmer until tender (one hour). Add water to maintain level. When chicken is tender, remove from pot. Take meat from bones. Slice bacon rolls and add to chicken meat. Put bones back into pot and boil thirty more minutes. Strain and add more seasoning, especially chili powder, if needed. Add cornstarch-water mixture and cook until it thickens. Put chicken and bacon into a serving dish. Add mushrooms and pour half of sauce over all. Sprinkle with almonds and serve. Pass remainder of sauce.

(Serves 6) **CIOPPINO**

Here is a stew that is popular in Italy and France wherever fish is found. Italian communities in the United States, especially on the West Coast and in Chicago, are well acquainted with it, too.

¼ cup olive oil
3 cloves garlic, minced
2 large onions, chopped
2 green peppers, chopped
1 can (16 ounces) tomatoes
1 can (8 ounces) tomato sauce
2 large bay leaves
¼ teaspoon oregano

¼ teaspoon pepper
½ teaspoon salt
2 cups dry white wine
2 lobster tails (8 ounces each)
1 pound sole or flounder
1 pound shrimp, shelled and cooked
1 can (6½ ounces) minced clams

Heat oil to sizzling in a large kettle and sauté garlic, chopped onions, and peppers until onion is soft and golden. Stir in tomatoes, tomato sauce, bay leaves, oregano, pepper, and salt. Chop tomatoes with a fork. Bring to boil. Reduce heat, cover, and simmer for forty minutes. Add wine and simmer ten more minutes. Shell lobster tails and cut into serving size pieces. Add lobster and sole or flounder to kettle. Cover and simmer another ten minutes. Stir in shrimp and minced clams. Heat through and serve with crusty French, Italian, or Vienna bread.

OSSO BUCCO *(Serves 4)*

This is one of the thriftiest gourmet dishes we know of. Be sure you buy **veal** shanks with lots of meat clinging to them, and also be sure to **dig out the** marrow from the bones after you've eaten the meat. The marrow is the thing with Osso Bucco!

4 veal shank bones
1 teaspoon salt
1 teaspoon black pepper
½ cup flour
3 tablespoons butter
1 tablespoon olive oil
2 garlic cloves, chopped
1 medium-sized onion, chopped

1 can (6 ounces) tomato paste
2 beef bouillon cubes, dissolved in 2/3 cup of water
2/3 cup dry white wine
1 anchovy fillet, chopped
4 tablespoons parsley, chopped
Grated rind of 1 lemon

Season shanks with salt and pepper and dredge in flour. Heat butter and olive oil in a large, heavy skillet and brown shanks over high heat on all sides. Add the garlic and onion and sauté five minutes. Mix the tomato paste with the bouillon and pour it and the wine over the shanks. Cover skillet tightly and simmer about one and a half hours (until meat is tender). Stir in the chopped anchovy.

Cook enough rice for four, adding a pinch of saffron to the water. Place rice on a serving platter and top with the shanks. Pour the sauce over all and top with the parsley and the lemon rind.

GREEN INFERNO

This is a treat for the coldest of winter days. It is such a hot stew that you would be well-advised to have a case of cold beer at tableside to consume before, during, and after eating.

2 pounds stewing beef, cut into 1½-inch cubes

2 tablespoons olive oil

1 teaspoon salt

2 beef bouillon cubes, dissolved in 1 cup boiling water

2 large onions, chopped

1 can (16 ounces) tomatoes

6 green chili peppers, cut into thin strips

2 cloves garlic, chopped

1 can (16 ounces) pinto or kidney beans, drained

Sauté beef in olive oil in a large kettle until golden brown on all sides. Stir in salt, bouillon, onions, tomatoes, chili peppers, and garlic. Bring to boil. Reduce heat, cover, and simmer two hours. Stir in beans, heat through, and serve.

JAMBALAYA *(Serves 4 to 6)*

From our own South comes the jambalayas, and they are a versatile stew mix of pork and fish as you wish. Our favorite jambalaya features shrimp and ham stewed in beer.

3 cups water
1 can stale beer
1½ teaspoons pickling spices
½ teaspoon salt
1 large bay leaf
1 pound raw shrimp
2 tablespoons butter
1 medium onion, chopped
1 clove garlic, minced

¾ cup raw (not instant) rice
2 chicken bouillon cubes, dissolved in 1 cup boiling water
3 drops Tabasco sauce
½ teaspoon chili powder
¼ teaspoon thyme
½ pound boiled ham, cut into strips
1 can (10 ounces) peas, drained
2 cans (6 ounces each) stewed tomatoes

Put water, half of the can of beer, pickling spices, salt, and bay leaf into kettle. Bring to boil and add shrimp. Cover and simmer for five minutes. Drain immediately and run cold water over the shrimp. Shell the shrimp and devein them.

Get butter sizzling in a large skillet and sauté onion and garlic until onion is soft. Stir in rice. Add chicken bouillon, remainder of the beer, Tabasco, chili powder, and thyme. Stir to blend. Bring to boil. Reduce heat, cover, and simmer twenty minutes (until rice is tender). Stir in shrimp, ham, peas, and tomatoes. Toss lightly with two forks. Heat through and serve immediately.

(Serves 4) AT THE TABLE

Very unusual and strictly for connoisseurs is this champagne-bathed stew from the private files of a New York publisher. You can prepare it at the table if you have an electric skillet or a chafing dish.

2 veal kidneys
2 tablespoons flour
4 tablespoons butter
1 pound fresh mushrooms, sliced into thirds
1 teaspoon salt
2 cups champagne
1 cup whipping cream
1 tablespoon chives, finely chopped

Removing connecting membranes and most of the visible fat on the kidneys. Cut into slices. Put flour on a sheet of waxed paper and dredge kidneys through it.

Heat butter to sizzling in a skillet and sauté kidney slices over high heat for two minutes, stirring frequently. Add mushrooms and sauté two more minutes, stirring frequently. Sprinkle with salt. Pour in one cup of champagne. Bring to a boil. Cover and simmer for eight minutes. Remove from heat and quickly stir in the cream and the remaining champagne. Return to heat and simmer for two more minutes. Sprinkle with chives and serve with rice.

PRIDE OF INDIA *(Serves 6)*

The famous Mulligatawny soups and stews originally came from India. Today they are served world-wide in varying degrees of thickness and in tastes from mild to hot. This recipe is an especially stewy Mulligatawny.

2 medium-sized onions
1 rib celery, diced
1 green pepper, diced
4 tablespoons butter
¼ teaspoon salt
¼ teaspoon pepper
4 tablespoons flour
2 tablespoons curry powder

¼ cup raw rice (not instant)
2 cans (8 ounces each) chicken broth
1 apple, peeled and diced
¼ small eggplant, peeled and diced
½ cup cooked chicken, diced
¼ cup sliced, toasted almonds
¼ teaspoon ground mace

Sauté onions, celery, and green pepper in butter in a stewing pan for ten minutes. Add salt, pepper, and flour, stirring to form a roux. Cook and stir one minute. Add curry powder and rice and slowly stir in the chicken broth. Mix well. Cover pan and simmer gently for one hour. Add diced apple and eggplant. Simmer 15 more minutes. Add chicken, almonds, and mace and simmer five minutes longer. Correct seasoning to taste and serve hot.

NOTE: You might want to add more water if you desire a thinner stew.

CARBONNADES A LA FLAMANDE

Last but certainly not the least in gourmet stews is Chef Sti Beauchard's Flemish dish, a creation using the very best features of Belgium's national stew. *(Serves 4)*

½ cup flour for dredging

Salt and freshly ground pepper to taste

2 pounds lean chuck, cut into 3-inch strips, ½-inch thick

1 large clove garlic, minced

¼ pound bacon, cut into 3-inch pieces

2 tablespoons butter

3 large onions, halved, finely sliced

1 teaspoon sugar

1 bay leaf

1 tablespoon white wine vinegar

1 slice bread, spread with 1 tablespoon Dijon mustard and cut into 1-in. squares

¼ teaspoon thyme

¼ teaspoon marjoram

2 tablespoons parsley, chopped fine

12 ounces dark beer

2 tablespoons butter

2 tablespoons flour

Combine one half cup flour, salt, and black pepper and dredge meat lightly. Heat bacon slices in skillet and cook until fat is transparent, not brown. Remove bacon and set to one side. Retain two tablespoons of bacon grease in skillet and add two tablespoons of butter to it. Heat shortening over medium flame and cook meat until it is brown on one side, and add onions. Cook until all the meat is brown and onions are lightly browned. Just before meat is ready to remove from the skillet, add garlic minced to meat-onion mixture, along with sugar and vinegar.

Butter a casserole dish lightly and form alternate layers of meat-onion mixture, the cut-up bread spread with mustard, and combined herbs, including the bay leaf. Add beer, cover, and place in a preheated 325-degree

(continued next page)

CARBONNADES A LA FLAMANDE

(Continued)

oven, baking until meat is tender (about two and half to three hours). About fifteen minutes before baking time is over, remove bay leaf and make a brown roux (a French word meaning "rusty") as follows:

Carefully brown two tablespoons of butter in top of double boiler over direct flame (until butter becomes slightly brown around the edges). Gradually blend in two tablespoons of flour, stirring until well combined, and remove from flame. Drain one cup of pan juice from the casserole and set to one side. Place butter-flour roux in its pan on top of double boiler and gradually add one cup of pan juice until a smooth sauce is formed. Return thickened sauce slowly into casserole until it reaches an agreeable degree of consistency, and then let casserole cook fifteen minutes longer. Serve with boiled potatoes on the side, beer, and a green salad.

WILD GAME STEWS

Practically everybody who deals in words has met Ernest Hemingway in a saloon in Paris, Havana, or Key West, Florida. But not everybody has heard the story about the kudu stew he made on one of his last safaris to Africa.

The story came out in a bull session on the subject of strength and how sad it was to see it decline in once-strong men as they grew older. The wind goes, the muscles slacken, enthusiasm wanes. All that was agreed upon. What couldn't be agreed upon was what was last to go, motor reflexes or the brain. As an answer, Hemingway was contemptible of either.

"I once knew a sports writer who used to say that the legs went first," he said over a daiquiri with shaved ice. "His name was Andy Farina and he worked for the old *News*. He was born without any fingers on his right hand, but he could write like an angel. You're damned right, an angel is what Andy Farina was. And he told me something else, too. He told me the last thing that goes in a man."

"The mind?"

"No."

Hemingway then told the story about the safari. He set out on it with a has-been of a fighter, Tommy Cisco, a character he'd found on the streets of Havana. It was a ninety-day safari paid for by Hemingway; forty-five dollars a day for a Jeep, a cook, gun bearers, trackers, and skinners. They shot their quota of bushbacks and bush cows and one rhino for the horns that the natives grind to powder to use as an aphrodasiac. They photographed zebra, antelope, and one of Africa's most vanishing species, a quagga. But what they really wanted was a greater kudu, the most challenging target of all safari enterprises.

"But Tommy's legs were bad," Hemingway said. "Soon we began to spend more time sacking in the tent than we did out on the game fields. And that was all right with the gun bearers and skinners because it gave them more time to swim and play touch football, a game they'd picked up from previous safaris and played with a mango.

" 'It's the legs, son,' Tommy said to me one day. 'It's the legs that go first.' I said to Tommy Cisco, 'I used to know a sports writer who believed the same thing, but I always said to him, 'For a fighter or a baseball player that may be true. But for a writer it's the mind that goes first. This sports writer I knew also told me what was the last to go.'

"Tommy thought a minute about this. Then he said, 'No, son, it's the legs that go first. Fighters, writers, all of them, it's the legs. Then it's the mind. And I know as well as your sports writer friend what's the last to go. It's the back and shoulders.'

"Well, just then we noticed a shadow loom in the opening of the tent. I was the first to see it, I guess. It was a male kudu about four hundred pounds with a good brown coat and fine corkscrew horns. Our rifles were on the other side of the tent. The kudu looked mean. We could hear the cook and the skinners and the rest playing down at the river where they'd gone for a swim, so we were alone. It was a bad moment. If we moved the kudu would leap and gore us with its corkscrew horns worse than a bull.

"While I was wondering what to do, Tommy Cisco jumped up on his painful legs and sprang at the kudu. He socked it square in the nose. The kudu went down on its knees like it had been hit with a hammer, and I got my rifle and shot it through the head. Cisco was a man, all right. His hands were fine and good. Both of them. They were like mallets.

"The rifle shot brought the safari crew back to the tent on the run. Before long we had a pot of water boiling and part of the skinned carcass of the kudu in it. Later we had a fine stew."

Hemingway looked up, and there was determination in his eyes, and pain, too. Behind his beard, he kind of grinned. "Now you see," he said. "It was just what Andy Farina always said. The last thing to go is heart."

At the time the authors heard this story they were more interested in what Hemingway had to say than in stew, so the ingredients that went into that kudu stew may never be known.

However, their interest in wild game stews probably was first awakened on that day. This chapter therefore is dedicated to Hemingway and to the hunters of the world — those men, and women, too, of heart, who can bring home a fresh rabbit or muskrat, a deer, a bear, or numerous other game animals and birds that are theirs for the asking.

In North America hunters aren't likely to find a kudu or any species that resembles it, although some people mistakenly claim that the pronghorn antelope that are popular game animals in the far west and Mexico are similar. The pronghorn is nothing like a kudu. It is of a group that is distinct from that to which the African antelope belongs.

The most hunted big game animal in America is the deer, since they are widely distributed and thrive in areas close to civilization. The most widely hunted small game animal is the rabbit. Between the two we have the popular elk, especially in the Rocky Mountain region where in the fall they come down from the high mountains for wintering. Moose are the hardest members of the deer family to hunt; they are not easily found, they travel fast, and they cover long distances. Caribou, the name by which the North American species of the reindeer is known, is a fast diminishing species, although they are still hunted with fervor in Canada and Alaska.

The most impressive North American big game animals are the Alaskan brown bear and the polar bear, and they also are the most dangerous. Both are extremely brutal when wounded, and will attack without provocation. Both have great powers of recovery. In our century hunting polar bears in Arctic America has become increasingly popular as a hobby, but it is an expensive one.

Other big game in North America includes mountain sheep and predators such as coyotes, foxes, and bobcats. On rare occasions jaguar and mountain lion (also known as cougar, panther, and puma) are found, and the surest way of hunting these cats is with a well-trained dog. Both are formidable enemies of dogs, however, and a too aggressive dog is apt to get hurt if it closes in too fast on one of these animals.

Wild boar and peccary also are hunted but, with peccaries especially, which live in caves and have sensitive snouts and ears, they are difficult to find. Wild boars are largely nocturnal and during the day retreat deep into cover. At dawn they are sometimes found feeding in the open. If a wild boar hunter sees nothing by nine o'clock in the morning, the hunt usually is finished for the day. Unlike bear and moose and other big game animals, these two are not purchaseable on the market.

Just as there are no wild boar or peccary stews known by the authors, neither are there any coyote, fox, or bobcat stews. Like dogs, these animals are rarely eaten by Americans. So in this chapter we will confine ourselves to those stewable animals, often obtainable at specialty stores for urbanites to whom hunting is as remote as a trip to the moon, such as rabbit, deer, moose, elk, arboreal rodents like the squirrel, and game birds like the pigeon.

As you can well imagine, wild game tends to be a little tougher than domesticated animals. For this reason it is important to cook wild meat slowly. Hot, or fast cooking, will make a good piece of game meat taste like plastic.

By the way, if you happen to pick up a good bear or venison steak and prefer to use it otherwise than in a stew, it would be a good idea to lard it well because it will tend to be lean and thus very dry.

BRER RABBIT *(Serves 4)*

Rabbit gets a head start in the wild game chapter because it is so plentiful. Here is a great stew for which you need only one of the small burrowing mammals.

1 rabbit, cleaned and deboned
2 tablespoons salt
4 tablespoons butter
3 large onions, chopped
2 cloves garlic, minced

1 rib celery, chopped
1 tablespoon paprika
½ cup water
½ cup sour cream

Cut rabbit meat into 1½-inch cubes and sprinkle with salt. Get butter sizzling in a kettle and add onions, garlic, and celery. Sauté until the onions are soft. Add rabbit pieces and paprika, stirring to coat rabbit well with the paprika. Add water. Bring to boil. Reduce heat, cover, and simmer for one and a half hours, until rabbit is tender. Add a little water from time to time if necessary. Remove from heat when rabbit pieces are tender. Stir in sour cream, one spoonful at a time. Return to stove, heat through (do not boil) and serve immediately.

(Serves 4) VINTAGE VENISON

Here is an old deer stew recipe that dates back to frontier days. Venison, by the way, is what the flesh of a deer that is used for food is called.

2 medium onions, grated
2 tablespoons butter
1½ pounds ground deer meat
1 cup bread crumbs
1 cup half and half
1 egg
1½ teaspoons cornstarch
1 teaspoon salt
½ teaspoon mace

¼ teaspoon nutmeg
4 tablespoons butter
2 tablespoons olive oil
3 tablespoons flour
2 cups dry red wine
2 beef bouillon cubes, dissolved in 1 cup of boiling water
1 teaspoon tomato paste
½ cup sour cream

Sauté onions in butter in a small skillet until onions are soft. In a mixing bowl, combine the onions with the ground meat, bread crumbs, cream, egg, cornstarch, salt, mace, and nutmeg. Knead mixture well and shape into balls about the diameter of a quarter.

Heat to sizzling the four tablespoons of butter and the olive oil in a large, heavy skillet. Sauté the meat balls for five minutes, turning often. Drain on paper towels and set to one side. Stir flour into skillet and cook and stir for one minute. Stir in wine, bouillon, and tomato paste and bring to a boil. Drop in meat balls. Cover skillet and simmer twenty minutes. Remove from heat and stir in sour cream, one spoonful at a time. Return to stove and heat through (but do not boil). Serve at once.

ONE BETTER *(Serves 4)*

Count Paul Stroganoff, the 19th century Russian diplomat who is credited with creating beef stroganoff, never had his mushrooms and sour cream with anything as good as deer meat. Here is a deer stroganoff he would have envied.

½ cup flour
1 tablespoon salt
1 teaspoon pepper
½ teaspoon cayenne pepper
2 pounds deer meat,
  cut into 1½-inch cubes
1 stick butter
2 cloves garlic, minced

1 large onion, chopped
2 chicken bouillon cubes, crushed
1 teaspoon Worcestershire sauce
1 bay leaf, crumbled
2 cups dry white wine
½ pound fresh mushrooms, sliced and
  sauteed in butter
1 cup sour cream

Put flour, salt, pepper, and cayenne pepper into a paper bag. Add meat cubes and shake to coat meat on all sides. Get butter sizzling hot in a large skillet. Add coated meat, garlic, and onion and sauté until meat is golden and the onion is soft. Add bouillon cubes, Worcestershire sauce, bay leaf, and wine. Scrape bottom of skillet with a spatula. Cover and simmer for thirty minutes. Meat should be tender. If not, simmer a bit more. When meat is tender remove from fire and stir in mushrooms and the sour cream, one spoonful at a time. Return to stove, heat through, and serve immediately.

And here is a moose stroganoff if you are lucky enough to bag the largest member of the deer family, or have a supplier. The name will fascinate your guests, and so will the taste.

*2 pounds moose meat,
cut into 1½-inch cubes
½ cup flour
2 teaspoons salt
1 teaspoon black pepper
½ teaspoon cayenne pepper
1 stick butter
1 medium-sized onion, chopped
2 cloves garlic, chopped*

*2 chicken bouillon cubes, crushed
1 can (4 ounces) button mushrooms
1 teaspoon Worcestershire sauce
1 bay leaf, crumbled
1 can (10½ ounces) cream of
celery soup
½ pint sour cream
Paprika*

Combine flour, salt, cayenne pepper, and pepper in a paper bag and toss moose cubes to coat well on all sides. Melt half a stick of butter in a large, heavy skillet and sauté meat until brown on all sides. Get remaining butter hot in another skillet and sauté onion and garlic until onion is soft. Combine all ingredients except the sour cream with the meat in the heavy skillet. Scrape bottom of skillet with a spatula. Cover and simmer one hour (until meat is tender). Add a little water during cooking if necessary. When meat is tender, stir in sour cream, one spoonful at a time. Heat through, sprinkle with paprika, and serve with noodles.

IT'S A SNAP *(Serves 6)*

We have trapped many a snapping turtle in bygone days. One thing we learned is that you must have a very large turtle to be able to enjoy turtle steaks, but as little as three pounds of turtle meat will make a delicious stew. Like this one.

3 pounds snapping turtle meat
2 tablespoons flour
¼ cup olive oil
3 medium-sized onions, chopped
2 cloves garlic, minced
3 cups water

½ cup dry Madeira wine
1 bay leaf, crumbled
½ teaspoon thyme
½ teaspoon salt
2 green onions, finely chopped

Cut turtle meat into 1½-inch cubes and sprinkle with the flour. Heat oil to sizzling in a saucepan and sauté onion and garlic until onion is soft. Add turtle meat and brown quickly on all sides over high heat. Stir in water and wine. Add bay leaf, thyme, and salt. Bring to a boil. Reduce heat, cover, and simmer for one hour (until meat is tender). Pour into soup bowls, sprinkle with the chopped green onions, and serve hot.

(Serves 4) HASENPFEFFER

Here is a classic German recipe for this universally favored rabbit stew, without which a stew cookbook would not be complete.

1 rabbit, fresh or frozen
½ cup red wine vinegar
3 cloves garlic, chopped
1 bay leaf, crumbled
2 teaspoons salt
1 teaspoon pepper
1 tablespoon mixed pickling spice

6 tablespoons olive oil
3 slices bacon, diced
2 medium onions, diced
1 bottle dry red wine, a fifth
12 tiny white onions, peeled
More salt and pepper to taste

Disjoint or have the rabbit disjointed. Wash and dry the pieces and set to one side. Put into a glass or earthenware bowl the vinegar, garlic, bay leaf, salt, pepper, pickling spice, and four tablespoons of the oil. Stir to blend. Add the rabbit pieces. Cover bowl and let marinate for forty-eight hours in the refrigerator. When ready to cook, drain the rabbit pieces.

Sauté bacon in a large pot or Dutch oven until crisp. Add onions and cook until soft. Stir in the flour, then add the rabbit pieces. Cook ten minutes, turning rabbit pieces to brown on all sides. Add the wine. Bring to a boil. Reduce heat, cover, and simmer one and one half hours (until rabbit is tender). Add salt and pepper to taste. While rabbit is cooking, sauté the little onions in remaining two tablespoons of oil until golden. Add onions to rabbit and serve hot with noodles on the side.

SQUIRRELY *(Serves 6)*

Second in popularity to the rabbit among small game hunters in America are the gray and red squirrels, which are shy and elusive little targets. Both marksmanship and woodcraft are tested in bagging them. If you should, here is an exceptionally squirrely stew to prepare.

3 squirrels, cleaned and cut
  into serving-size pieces
4 tablespoons salt in pot of boiling water
6 slices lean bacon
1½ gallons boiling water
6 small potatoes, boiled and diced
2 carrots, scraped and diced

1 rib celery, diced
1 can (12 ounces) kernel corn
1 can (8 ounces) lima beans
2 tomatoes, chopped
½ head cabbage, grated
½ teaspoon salt
½ teaspoon pepper

Place pieces of squirrel in salted, boiling water, and parboil briskly for fifteen minutes. Drain meat, then add, along with the bacon, to the 1½ gallons of boiling water in a large kettle. Simmer for one and a half hours (until meat loosens from bones). Remove meat from bones and return to pot. Add potatoes, carrots, and celery and simmer, covered, until vegetables are tender. Add all other ingredients, cover, and simmer ten more minutes. Taste for seasoning and serve hot.

Ireland, already justly famous for its stews, also claims a great one made from rabbit, which they used to think of as the poor man's chicken. A plague hit the rabbit warrens about twenty years ago and virtually wiped out the rabbit population, but being prolific they are now making a comeback. Here's how they make an Irish rabbit stew.

1 young rabbit
1 tablespoon white vinegar
2 carrots, scraped and sliced
2 medium-sized onions, sliced thin
2 ribs celery, chopped
2 medium-sized potatoes, sliced thin

2 turnips, scraped and sliced
6 slices lean bacon, minced
1 bay leaf, crumbled
¼ teaspoon thyme
3 tablespoons parsley, chopped
½ teaspoon pepper

Cut rabbit into serving-size pieces and soak them for an hour in a bowl of water to which vinegar has been added. Wipe rabbit pieces dry and set to one side.

Arrange half of the vegetables in layers on the bottom of a large stewing pan. Add the rabbit pieces and sprinkle with the minced bacon. Layer on the remainder of the vegetables and sprinkle with bay leaf, thyme, parsley, and pepper. Add just enough water to come to the top of the vegetables. Cover tightly and simmer gently for one and a half hours. When rabbit is tender, stir the stew well and serve immediately.

COTTONTAIL *(Serves 4)*

Here is one more rabbit stew, more American than either Irish or German, easier to make than Hasenpfeffer but still exotic with its addition of garlic and mushrooms.

1 rabbit, fresh or frozen
3 tablespoons butter
2 teaspoons salt
1 teaspoon pepper
2 tablespoons flour
1 chicken bouillon cube, dissolved
in ¼ cup boiling water

½ cup dry white wine
4 slices lean bacon, diced
2 cloves garlic, minced
12 tiny white onions, peeled
½ pound fresh mushrooms,
* sliced into thirds*

Cut rabbit into pieces, and wash and dry the pieces. Melt butter in a large pot or Dutch oven and quickly brown the rabbit pieces on all sides. Sprinkle with salt, pepper, and flour, and cook three more minutes, stirring to blend the flour. Pour in the bouillon and wine. Bring to boil. Reduce heat, cover, and cook forty-five minutes. While rabbit is cooking, brown bacon in a skillet. Pour off half of the drippings and sauté the garlic and onions until soft. Add mushrooms and sauté two more minutes. Add bacon-mushroom mixture to the rabbit and cook fifteen more minutes (until rabbit is tender). Skim off the fat and serve hot with noodles on the side.

TAKE YOUR PICK

Goulash, or "herdsman's meat," is not made only with beef or veal and vegetables. Game also can be used. For this one you may select deer, elk, or moose meat.

1½ pounds boneless deer,
elk, or moose meat
½ cup flour
4 tablespoons butter
1 large onion, chopped
½ teaspoon salt

1 tablespoon paprika
2 beef bouillon cubes, dissolved
in 1 cup boiling water
4 potatoes, peeled and quartered
4 carrots, cut into 2-inch pieces

Cut meat into two-inch cubes and dredge in the flour. Melt butter in kettle and sauté meat until brown on all sides. Add onion and continue cooking until soft. Stir in salt and paprika and scrape bottom of kettle with a spatula. Pour in bouillon. Bring to boil, reduce heat, cover, and simmer one and a half hours (meat should be almost tender). Add potatoes and carrots and simmer thirty more minutes. If necessary, add a little more water during cooking to maintain original liquid level.

PAPA BEAR *(Serves 6)*

Bear meat *is* different. If you are lucky enough to have a specialty butcher shop in your area, then by all means try this stew which is a prized dish at big game lodges everywhere. This recipe comes from the Winnipeg area of Canada.

3 pounds bear meat, cut into 1½-inch cubes
1 tablespoon salt
2 teaspoons pepper
½ cup flour
1 cup cooking oil
1 cup water
1 bay leaf

¼ teaspoon thyme
2 tablespoons parsley, chopped
2 cups dry red wine
6 carrots, scraped and cut in half
6 onions, peeled
6 turnips, peeled
6 potatoes, peeled and quartered.

Remove fat from meat and cut into cubes. Put salt, pepper, and flour in a paper bag. Add meat cubes and shake well to coat all sides.

Get oil sizzling hot in a heavy pot and quickly sear cubes of bear meat on all sides. Add water, bay leaf, thyme, parsley, and wine. Bring to a boil. Reduce heat, cover, and simmer for three and a half hours. Add vegetables and a little more water, if necessary. Cook another thirty minutes (until vegetables are done), and serve immediately.

THE STRANGE ONES

To understand the origin of some of the unusual stews to be found in this chapter (like the pickle stew from Russia or the prune stew from the Balkans) it is necessary to go back in time about two hundred and seventy-five years.

That was just before the close of the eighteenth century when an economic pessimist named Thomas Robert Malthus published a very funny book in England. The title was a whopper: *An Essay on the Principles of Population as it Affects the Future Improvements of Society, with remarks on the Speculations of Mr. Godwin, M. Condorcet, and Other Writers.*

Eppa Fiss McGow, as the book is called nowadays after its initials, was a lousy book written by a poor thinker. But it contained the germ of an idea that electrified Malthus' generation and put a brake on the prevailing economic enthusiasm of the time. And too bad for the inner city people then, the poor, the overworked, and the maimed, the idea was so persuasive that it also ushered in an era of low wages, emasculated the idea of charity, and completely crippled social reform for the next century.

The idea, or theory Malthus propounded, was a neat one which many people still believe today under another name, the population explosion. Malthus said in essence that no matter how plentiful the food of any one country may be, population will outstrip the supply, with no limit to that population's ratio of increase except war, pestilence, or "vice." "Vice" was Malthus' Victorian term for contraceptives.

As more advanced economists since have learned, Malthus never skillfully set out his premises for that argument, nor did he examine their logical status. Neither did his handling of factual data ever reach any high degree of sophistication. For example, nowhere in Eppa Fiss McGow is there a mention of stew, when as a matter of record it can be said that stew by itself refutes Malthus. To put it another way, in an anti-Malthusian way: in all societies inventiveness with stew tends to outpace population growth, so that the size of the family in such societies is dependent only on the diversity of stews those families can invent.

Now we catch a glimpse of why the strange stews you are about to sample came into being.

They grew out of a divine contempt for the logic of economic law. The authors of *The Stew Cookbook* can state this no more vividly than did a theatrical group in Detroit, The Casualty Players, in a little tour de force they performed called "Back to Malthusia."

In the play, two actors named Gurd and Gun sat crouched on the stage before a bonfire over which a pot of vegetables was boiling. They conversed like savages, by intonation, their ideas communicated on a chromatic scale (we still use this language with our dogs).

The size of Gurd and Gun's family was immense and growing (Gun was pregnant and she was eating handfuls of fertility herbs throughout the play). Savage children filled the stage, clamoring, by intonation, their want of food. Gurd and Gun, by now alarmed, conveyed the idea that the pot of vegetables would not feed them all. So the mother and father began looking for other items of food to throw into the pot. Gun found some nuts and berries and mushrooms; Gurd found a fish; Gun discovered some milk that had soured. Licking it, she found it tasteworthy. It, too, went into the pot. The comic high point was reached when Gurd appeared with a ten-gallon can of Van Camp's pork and beans. After emptying it into the pot he stuck his head in the can to see if there were any more beans, and got his head stuck. He suffocated and died as the curtain went down on the first act.

"Back to Malthusia's" second act was a paean to man's ability to overcome hardship and somehow survive in a hostile world. Gun's children had been born; meanwhile, she'd found another savage to marry. Stews boiled everywhere on the stage. There was a festival and a fair. Over in one corner a philosopher was holding forth to a group of Gun's children. A garbageman appeared for the first time in the play, shoveling the family's leavings into a pail. In a word, the play seemed to say that All follows Stew.

This chapter will attempt to say the same thing. As earlier, we found the bread of mankind in the plenty of their ordinary years, here we will find the bread of mankind in the agony of their leaner years. For it is a truism that stews are both a luxury and a poverty food. When there was a surplus, that surplus would be turned into stew; likewise, when a bad year came along and the land was leaner, whatever was available was made into a stew, thus stretching existing stores. The prune stew was invented early in the seventeenth century when the Austro-Hungarian empire of the Hapsburgs got the worst in a barter deal with the Ukraine, and for fabrics and spices imported from the East got more plums than the nation could consume. And the pickle stew was invented in the 1880s during one of Russia's great famines.

These eccentric sparks from the flintstone of the stew wheel are the subject of this chapter.

Are you in a pickle for something different to serve? Try pickle and kidney stew, originally a Russian treat called Rassolnik. You may call it anything you like as long as you are kind, because it is delicious.

1 large beef kidney
1 quart beef consomme
1 quart water
1 teaspoon dill weed, chopped
2 cups onions, diced
2 tablespoons butter
2 cups red potatoes, diced

2 medium dill pickles, diced
½ cup pickle juice
1½ teaspoons salt
1½ teaspoons sugar
¼ teaspoon black pepper
1 tablespoon chives, chopped
sour cream

Boil kidney in water to cover for forty-five minutes. Remove, rinse, and cut into quarters lengthwise. Remove membrane and slice one-eighth inch thick. Put into large pot with the consomme, water, and dill. Sauté diced onions until soft in the butter in a skillet. Add onions, potatoes, pickles, and pickle juice, to pot. Cover and boil for thirty minutes. Add salt, sugar, and pepper. Toss in the chives. Serve hot with a dollop of sour cream floating on each serving if you desire.

PRUNE *(Serves 6)*

Everybody laughed when prunes, the funny fruit, were mentioned. But they really roared at the idea of prune stew. However, believe it or not, here it is and it is really great.

¼ cup onions, chopped
¼ cup butter
2 pounds beef, cut into 1½-inch cubes
1 teaspoon salt
¼ teaspoon pepper

1 jar (16 ounces) pitted prunes
4 whole cloves
1 teaspoon cinnamon
1 can (15 ounces) yam halves, drained

Sauté onions in butter until onions are soft. Add beef and brown on all sides. Add salt and pepper. Cover and simmer gently for fifteen minutes. Add prunes, with juice, and cloves, cinnamon, and yams. Cover and simmer thirty more minutes (until meat is tender). Serve immediately.

TRIPE

Cheap and wildly nutritious, this one is a version of Pepper Pot stew and uses tripe as one of the main ingredients. It's a hearty dish good for cold winter nights or hot summer nights, whichever you will.

3 slices bacon, diced
2 medium onions, chopped
1 large green pepper, chopped
2 beef bouillon cubes
2 quarts water
1 bay leaf, crumbled
1 teaspoon pepper

½ teaspoon salt
1/8 teaspoon thyme
¼ teaspoon cayenne pepper
½ pound honeycomb tripe, cut into cubes
3 medium potatoes, peeled and diced
3 tablespoons butter
3 tablespoons flour

Fry the diced bacon in a large stew pot until crisp. Add the onion and green pepper and sauté until the onion is soft. Add the bouillon cubes, water bay leaf, pepper, salt, thyme, cayenne, tripe, and diced potatoes. Bring to boil. Reduce heat, cover, and simmer one hour. Blend together the butter and flour and dilute it with a bit of broth from the pot. Quickly stir into the pot and continue simmering until stew thickens. Serve immediately.

FRANKFURTER *(Serves 6)*

Hot dog, here's one the kids are sure to love. It goes all the way with hominy, stuffed olives, and cheddar cheese, and really isn't as strange as it sounds.

1/3 cup olive oil
2 medium onions, sliced thin
1 clove garlic, minced
6 frankfurters, sliced into quarters
1 can (16 ounces) kidney beans and juice
1 can (16 ounces) hominy, drained

1½ teaspoons chili powder
2 cups tomato juice
½ cup stuffed olives, sliced
½ cup cheddar cheese, diced
4 slices Italian or French bread, spread with butter

Heat olive oil to sizzling in a large, heavy skillet. Sauté onions and garlic until onions are soft. Add frankfurter slices and brown lightly. Add the kidney beans and juice, the hominy, chili powder, tomato juice, and olives. Heat to boiling, add cheese, and immediately remove from heat. Pour into a shallow baking dish (12 x 7½ x 2). Arrange bread slices on top. Slip into a 400-degree preheated oven until bread is lightly browned, and serve immediately.

(Serves 6) EGGPLANT

How do you like your eggplant? How about in a stew with fish? It may sound like a strange combination, but there is nothing strange about the mouth-watering taste.

1 large onion, diced
2 large tomatoes, peeled and chopped
1 small eggplant, peeled and diced
1 large green pepper, diced
2 large radishes, sliced thin but not peeled
3 cups boiling water

1 tablespoon salt
½ teaspoon pepper
¼ teaspoon cayenne pepper
1 pound any white fish
2 cloves garlic, minced
1 tablespoon lemon juice

Into a three-quart pot put onion, tomatoes, eggplant, green pepper, radishes, boiling water, and salt. Bring to a boil. Reduce heat, cover, and simmer for fifteen minutes. Mix black pepper and cayenne and rub it into both sides of the fish. Add to the stew along with the garlic and lemon juice. Cover and simmer about ten minutes (until fish is flaky, not mushy), and serve immediately.

BUTTERMILK AND RAISINS *(Serves 4)*

Did somebody say buttermilk and raisins? In a stew? Yes. It's a very old favorite with the great Danes of Copenhagen's countryside and we think you will like it, too.

4 tablespoons butter
4 tablespoons flour
1 quart buttermilk
½ cup raisins, plumped for 10 minutes in hot water and drained
2 lemon slices
2 egg yolks
¾ cup sugar

Melt butter in a two-quart saucepan. Blend in flour and cook and stir for two minutes. Add buttermilk, a trickle at a time, stirring constantly to keep it from curdling. Remove from heat and add raisins and lemon slices. Beat the eggs and sugar together until fluffy, add to the stew, heat through (but do not boil), and serve.

(Serves 4) MUSKRAT

Muskrat and beaver are popular meats in Minnesota, and they should be, for the meat is about as sweet as anything we've ever tasted, reflecting their diets made up exclusively of marsh roots and clams. If you find muskrat hard to get, talk to your furrier. He may help you.

Hind legs from 8 muskrats
1 quart water
4 tablespoons butter
1 medium-sized onion, sliced
1½ teaspoons nutmeg
1 cup celery and leaves finely sliced
Salt and pepper to taste
1/3 cup white wine

Clean the fat from the muskrat legs (or hams) and boil in salted water for forty-five minutes.

In a deep-sided braising skillet melt the butter and add the sliced onion, cooking until the onion is lightly browned. Set aside.

Remove muskrat from water, dry with a paper towel, and sprinkle nutmeg over hams, rubbing in well. Place seasoned hams in skillet and brown well over and evenly over medium heat. Add onions, celery and leaves, and salt and pepper to taste. Then add wine, turn heat down low, and simmer for thirty minutes. Serve with rice.

TURNIP *(Serves 4)*

A book could be written about this strange and delicious vegetable root which is cultivated almost everywhere in the world. Instead of a book, we will give you a stew, and it is a very hot stew indeed.

½ pound stewing beef, cut into 1-inch cubes
2 cups water
2 tablespoons olive oil
2 medium-sized onions, chopped
3 chili peppers, ground

½ pound finnan haddie
3 tomatoes, chopped
1 medium-sized turnip, ground
water

Put cut-up beef into a kettle with two cups of water and boil until the meat is tender. Heat the olive oil in a skillet and add the chopped onions, cooking until the onions turn transparent. Add the ground chili peppers and finnan haddie cut into bite-sized pieces and cook for two minutes. Add tomatoes and cook ten minutes more. Add the beef and broth it cooked in and boil for five minutes. Add the ground turnip and cook over low flame for about twenty more minutes, adding water for desired consistency. Serve hot with rice.

From Venice comes this original way to take a lot of beans and work them up into an excellent old world type of stew.

1 pound dry white or red beans
1 tablespoon shortening
4 slices bacon, diced
1 medium onion, diced
1 clove garlic, diced
1 rib celery, diced

1 can (8 ounces) tomatoes
1 teaspoon salt
½ teaspoon black pepper
3 cups hot water
1/8 pound romano cheese, grated

Soak beans overnight. Rinse well and cover with water. Simmer two hours. Drain and set to one side.

Melt shortening in a large pan. Add bacon, onions, garlic, and celery, and cook until onions are golden. Add tomatoes, salt, pepper, water, and beans. Cover and simmer for twenty minutes. Ladle into bowls, sprinkle generously with cheese, and serve.

STEWS AROUND THE WORLD

Like everybody else, the authors of *The Stew Cookbook* have heard the expression "perpetual stew" all of their lives. Usually it designated what a fuss-budget or a shillyshallerer put people into by fussing too much over trifles. It wasn't until the authors reached Heidelberg, Germany, that they ever knew anything like a Perpetual Stew ever existed.

There they met a man named Martin Stockenhauser who worked at three jobs but still was always broke. His wife begged him to be allowed to take care of the money, promising that if she did she would put the family on a paying basis. One day the overworked husband agreed and the wife immediately cooked up a pot of stew, saying, "To begin with, we are going to eat to live in this family, not live to eat." Each day she added something new to the leftover stew, thereby inventing the *Perpetual Stew* that helped put the family in the black. The recipe for the origin of her stew will be found in this chapter under the title *Heidelberg*.

Likewise, the authors always knew that hippopotamuses could swim, but elephants, hardly. However, in their travels around the world looking for stews they saw an elephant do just that in Barranquilla, Colombia.

It happened when a circus elephant fell into the swimming pool at the Hotel Del Prado during a particularly boisterous festival celebrating the hotel's centennial. Waves of water cascaded over the poolside loungers and spread to the cantina where we were dining on *Centennial Stew.* As the elephant treaded water, bellowing mightily through its trunk, we watched the rescue efforts which included a crane, an improvised stretcher made from a trampoline canvas, and swarms of little brown men running around and shouting as though it were the start of a revolution. The recipe for that *Centennial Stew* will be found in this chapter under the title *Barranquilla*.

As could have been predicted, it was in the Orient that the authors ran into the most difficulty in finding stew recipes, although Orientals, and especially the Chinese, are world renowned for their stews. But the recipes for them are much harder to come by than merely sitting in a cantina watching an elephant flounder in a hotel swimming pool. For one thing, it is almost impossible, because of the language barrier, for a Westerner to walk into an ordinary restaurant, find a stew and eat it, and then make the cook understand that you would be honored to share the recipe. For another, Orientals almost always insist upon taking Westerners to a special room where they put on a feast which rarely includes a stew.

But in Hong Kong we ran into Jacques Berrault, a correspondent for *Le Figaro* in Paris, who was on his way out of Red China, and together we talked our way into a Vei-Shou, an ordinary restaurant with hundreds of bicycles parked outside. There we had a stew made with Chinese noodles and chicken, and Jacques helped us get the recipe from the cook. The recipe will be found in this chapter under the title *Hong Kong*.

We have crossed oceans and climbed mountains looking for foreign stews. We have spent footpower and lungpower, ridden asses in Greece and donkey carts in India. But no expedition in search of a stew was more dangerous than one we made in Argentina when we went along on a ten-mile cattle drive over the pampas in a blinding snowstorm.

It was July, and we had every right to expect a warm summer day. But on the other side of the equator, where even our shadows surprised us by falling on the wrong side of our bodies, July can be as fierce as a December day in Iceland, or in Chicago.

The drive began, and the old lead cow struck out immediately, taking first place from the others who were strung out behind her for almost a quarter of a mile. The snow thickened; small, dry flakes from the dark Antarctic, falling straight down. There was no growth in this region of the pampas but some bare trees along the creek bottoms. The snow heaped on the curly rumps all around us. Calves fell in the hard going, their flanks rising and falling. We lifted them back on their feet and held them a moment, knocking off the snow and ice and giving them a shove to send them on their way.

The journey, that should have taken four hours, took all day. The lead cow never stopped; she was busy breaking the trail to the stock pens where she and the herd would be quartered for the winter. She passed over a hill and struck a drift, sinking to her shoulders. The entire procession slowed noticeably. Then she trampled her way through the drift, breasted the hill, never halting, and the stream of cows followed through the path she trampled out for them.

It was nighttime before the snow stopped and we glimpsed the squares of yellow light that marked off the cattle's wintering grounds. In a commotion of moos and repeated bawls from the calves, we loosened the cinches and dragged the saddles off our horses' backs. We measured out oats and fed them. Then we swung sacks of hay and feed onto a wagon and began circling the pen, breaking open the sacks and emptying them in the wagon's wake. Only after another endless amount of time was the job done and we headed for the house.

How good that rude shelter of a cabin looked to us who had eaten nothing since breakfast. It was boiling with heat and on the stove the stew we had been promised was simmering. We peeled off layers of clothing down to our saggy-kneed longjohns. And when we were ready, our plates were heaped with stew and bread, smoking coffee setting beside them, and we ate, saying nothing. We just ate and ate and ate until everything was gone, and then we crawled to our bunks across the room and slept and slept and slept until not a muscle remained that had any fatigue left in it. The stew we had that night will be found in this chapter under the title *Buenos Aires*.

And so it went. In compiling the recipes for this chapter there has been both agony and joy. There also has been expense. Often when we have set out, in tandem or alone, to obtain a recipe for a special stew that we must at all costs have, when by plane, train, boat, and finally taxi we arrive at the holy of holies and by sheer weight of pleading and persuasion (and often bribery) get the recipe we came for, we are reminded of the old Hungarian saying: "We wish we could afford to live the way we do."

But then those bad times pass and by some miracle we are solvent again. The vibrant stew spirit awakens, and we are off. To the plains and forests of Hungary next? Yes, let's go!

But that will be for another book.

HAVANA *(Serves 4)*

A doctor who fled Cuba gave us this recipe for an authentic Havana stew. In addition to olive oil and tomatoes which are often used in stews, this one features finely chopped seedless raisins which give it a special lift.

2 large onions, chopped fine
1 large green pepper, chopped
2 cloves garlic, minced
¼ cup olive oil
1 pound lean beaf, minced
1 can (16 ounces) peeled tomatoes
¼ teaspoon oregano

½ teaspoon salt
½ teaspoon black pepper
1 tablespoon capers, drained
1 tablespoon cider vinegar
¼ cup pimento stuffed olives, chopped
½ cup seedless raisins, finely chopped

Sauté onions, green pepper, and garlic in hot olive oil in a large, heavy skillet, until onions are soft. Add minced beef and stir it with a fork until it becomes lightly browned. Add tomatoes together with juice. Break up tomatoes with a fork and blend with the meat. Add remainder of the ingredients, stirring in well. Simmer, covered, for one hour. Skim off any grease that has risen to the surface. Serve hot with fluffy rice.

It wasn't in Warsaw, after all, that we found the best Polish stew. It was in Cracow, in a "Ma and Pa" cafe on a side street which, Polish street names being what they are, has long since been forgotten.

2½ pounds sauerkraut
1 pound fresh mushrooms, sliced
4 strips lean bacon, diced
1 large onion, chopped
2 tablespoons parsley, minced
2 tablespoons flour
2 pounds round steak,
cut into 1½-inch cubes

1 garlic sausage, sliced
2 beef bouillon cubes,
dissolved in
1 cup boiling water
½ teaspoon salt
½ teaspoon pepper
2 tablespoons sugar
½ cup dry red wine

Rinse sauerkraut in cold water and put it into a large kettle with the mushrooms. Cover tightly and simmer gently for fifteen minutes. Meanwhile, sauté bacon, onion, and parsley in a skillet until the onions are soft. Stir in flour and cook one minute, stirring frequently. Add to sauerkraut in the kettle. Put beef cubes and sausage into the skillet and sauté until the beef is lightly browned. Stir the browned beef and sausage into kettle and add bouillon, salt, pepper, and sugar. Stir to blend well. Cover and bake in a 300-degree oven for one and one fourth hours (until meat is tender). Stir in wine, heat through, and serve hot.

AMSTERDAM *(Serves 5 to 6)*

Here is a Dutch stew we enjoyed eating in a small restaurant near the Central Station, just outside the Sailors' Quarter in swinging Amsterdam. Let us caution you to be sure to leave your beer open an hour or two before adding it to the stew.

4 slices lean bacon, minced
2 medium onions, sliced thin
2 pounds round steak, cut into 1½-inch cubes
1 teaspoon salt
½ teaspoon pepper
1½ tablespoons flour

2 cans stale beer
1 bay leaf, crumbled
¼ teaspoon thyme
2 cloves garlic, minced
1 tablespoon sugar
1 teaspoon white vinegar

Cook bacon in a large, heavy skillet until it is crisp. Put bacon bits into a heavy earthenware pot. Sauté onions in skillet until they are soft and then add to pot. Put beef cubes into skillet and brown lightly on all sides. Sprinkle with salt, pepper and flour, and stir until the flour is absorbed by the meat. Stir in the beer, scraping bottom of the skillet with a spatula. Blend well, then add to pot along with bay leaf, thyme, garlic, sugar, and vinegar. Stir to blend. Cover tightly and bake one and a half hours in a 325-degree oven (until meat is tender), and serve immediately.

The French are noted for many types of stews, the daube being one of them. This one was enjoyed on a cool late September day at a very French restaurant at Grasse in the hills behind Nice.

4 strips lean bacon, chopped
¼ teaspoon allspice
3 garlic cloves, cut into slivers
4 pound chuck roast
3 cups dry red wine
1 cup olive oil
2 teaspoons salt
½ teaspoon thyme

1½ teaspoons black pepper
2 tablespoons grated lemon peel
¼ cup flour
1 bay leaf, crumbled
8 small white onions, peeled
8 small carrots, scraped and cut into 1-inch pieces
8 small new potatoes, peeled and quartered

Sprinkle bacon with the allspice. Make small slits in the meat with a sharp knife and force the pieces of bacon and slivers of garlic into the slits. Put meat into a shallow dish and pour wine over it. Let it marinate for two hours at room temperature, turning occasionally. Drain meat and save the marinade.

Heat the oil in a heavy skillet and sear the meat on both sides over high heat. Add the salt, thyme, pepper, and lemon peel, and flour. Stir to blend. Pour in the marinade, plus enough water to make three cups of liquid. Sprinkle in the bay leaf. Cover and simmer on top of stove for three and one half hours. Add vegetables and more water, if needed, and simmer covered another thirty minutes (until vegetables are done), and serve immediately.

LONDON *(Serves 6)*

The English, of course, don't only have steak and kidney pies. They also have steak and kidney stews and here is one we ate at the inn across the road from the entrance to Hampton Court.

1 pound beef kidneys
2 tablespoons salt in 2 quarts cold water
2 tablespoons butter
3 pounds round steak, cut into ½-inch cubes
1 large onion, chopped
1 pound fresh mushrooms, sliced

1 cun water
Salt and pepper to taste
1 teaspoon Worcestershire sauce
2 tablespoons flour
½ cup dry sherry

Soak kidneys in salted water for an hour. Drain, split, and remove fat and the large tubes. Slice crosswise into one-half-inch pieces. Get butter sizzling in a large skillet and brown kidneys and steak for two minutes, stirring frequently. Add onion, mushrooms and water. Cover and simmer thirty minutes. Add salt and pepper to taste and then the Worcestershire sauce. Stir in the flour and the sherry and blend well. Simmer ten more minutes and serve over toasted English muffin halves.

(Serves 4) # BUDAPEST

The proprietor of the small restaurant where we had this wonderful stew, or goulash, came from Szeged, a small town in the center of the finest paprika growing fields in the world. She used Szeged paprika exclusively in her cooking, and it left a delicious aftertaste.

1½ pounds shoulder of veal
2 large onions, chopped
1 tablespoon lard
½ teaspoon sugar
1 tablespoon paprika

1 medium tomato, chopped
1 medium green pepper, chopped
1½ cups water
1 teaspoon salt

Cut veal into one-half-inch cubes. Cook onions until soft in the lard in a heavy skillet. Stir in the sugar. Add the meat and simmer for fifteen minutes. Add paprika, tomato, green pepper, water and salt. Stir to blend. Cover tightly and simmer for one hour. Do not under any circumstances lift the lid during the cooking time. When finished, serve immediately with noodles.

EDINBURGH *(Serves 4)*

As though nobody knew, let us repeat that the Scotch are a thrifty bunch, and so make the most of stews. This one, made with lamb shanks, is popular in the Edinburgh area.

1 tablespoon lard
4 lamb shanks
2 quarts water
¼ cup raw barley
1 large onion, sliced thin

2 tablespoons parsley, chopped
2 ribs celery, chopped, leaves and all
2 teaspoons salt
4 medium-sized potatoes, peeled and quartered

Melt lard in a large, heavy skillet. Brown the shanks on all sides in the lard. Add the water, barley, onions, parsley, celery, and salt. Cover, bring to a boil, reduce heat, and simmer for one and a half hours. Add potatoes and continue cooking for thirty minutes (until potatoes are done). Remove lamb shanks and take the meat from the bones. Cut meat into bite-size pieces. Return it to the stew, heat through, and serve immediately.

(Serves 6) # BARRANQUILLA

Here is the recipe for our memorable Centennial Stew. In it you will note that the Colombian cook who made it pulled out all stops in putting it together.

2 pounds boiling beef, cut into 1½-inch cubes
1 bay leaf, crumbled
½ teaspoon cumin seed
6 black peppercorns
½ teaspoon garlic salt
2 teaspoons salt
1½ teaspoons cider vinegar
1 quart water

2 medium-sized potatoes
2 large carrots
4 ribs celery, chopped
1 large onion, sliced thin
2 tomatoes, diced
¼ teaspoon saffron
½ teaspoon ground oregano
¾ cup fresh shelled peas

Into a three-quart stew pot put the beef, bay leaf, cumin seed, peppercorns, garlic, salt, cider vinegar, and water. Bring to boil. Reduce heat, cover, and simmer for one hour. Peel potatoes and scrape carrots and cut both potatoes and carrots into one-inch pieces. Add potatoes, carrots, celery, onion slices, and tomatoes to the pot. Cover and cook another twenty minutes. Mix saffron and oregano in one teaspoon of water and add to the pot, along with the peas. Simmer five more minutes, and serve immediately.

PANAMA CITY *(Serves 6 to 8)*

There are so many bananas in Panama that some way had to be found to keep them from getting ripe at the same time. Thus this green banana stew. Make sure the bananas are green, though, or it won't work.

2 pounds pork shoulder,
  cut into 1½-inch cubes
1 pound lean beef, cut into 1½-inch cubes
6 slices boiled ham, diced
1 tablespoon salt
1 bay leaf, crumbled
4 cups water
1 small onion, minced
3 tablespoons fresh lime juice

2½ cups potatoes, diced
2 cups yellow squash
½ cup parsley, chopped
1 whole garlic sausage, sliced
1 teaspoon pepper
1 teaspoon ground coriander
¼ teaspoon cayenne pepper
2 green bananas,
  cut into ½-inch slices

Put pork, beef, and ham into a large stew pot. Add salt, bay leaf, and water. Bring to boil. Reduce heat, cover, and simmer for one and one half hours. Add minced onion, lime juice, potatoes, squash, parsley, sausage, pepper, coriander, and cayenne. Cover and simmer fifteen more minutes. Add banana slices and simmer another ten minutes, and serve immediately.

From "the top of the hill" in the old Greek town of Rhodes comes this luncheon specialty stew. It's the attraction three times a week at a small restaurant there.

2 pounds beef, cut into 1½-inch cubes
4 tablespoons olive oil
2 cups water
1 can (6 ounces) tomato paste
3 tablespoons red wine vinegar
2 teaspoons salt

½ teaspoon sugar
½ teaspoon pepper
1 teaspoon garlic salt
2 cinnamon sticks
10 whole cloves
2 pounds small white onions, peeled

Brown beef cubes in olive oil in large stew pot. In a mixing bowl combine the water, tomato paste, wine vinegar, salt, sugar, pepper, and garlic salt. Stir to blend and pour over meat. Add cinnamon sticks. Stick the cloves into one of the onions and add to pot. Bring to boil. Reduce heat, cover, and simmer for one and one half hours (until meat is tender). Add remaining onions and cook until they are tender (about fifteen minutes). Remove cinnamon sticks and the onion with the cloves, and serve.

DUBROVNIK *(Serves 6)*

A small restaurant on one of the "step streets" behind the main street of old Dubrovnik provided this Yugoslavian, or Serbian, cabbage stew. Its flavor is surpassed only by its ability to nourish.

2 pounds lamb stew meat
1 cup lard
1 large onion, chopped
1 or 2 cabbages (4 pounds in all)
3 cups water
½ teaspoon salt

4 tomatoes, sliced
½ teaspoon black pepper
5 cloves garlic, minced
1 tablespoon flour
1 teaspoon paprika

Cut meat into one and one half inch cubes. Get half a cup of the lard hot in a skillet and brown meat on all sides. Add chopped onion and continue cooking until onion is soft. Remove outer leaves of the cabbage and cut the cabbage head into fairly big pieces. Arrange the cabbage and meat in layers in a casserole. Add water, salt, tomato slices, pepper, and garlic. Cover and simmer two to three hours over a low heat. Add a bit of water from time to time. When the meat is tender, mix the flour and paprika with the remaining lard and stir gently into the stew. When the stew thickens, serve immediately.

In Armenia, the oldest Christian state, they say the best way to conclude a bargain is over a good bowl of stew. And we found one in the capital city of Erivan.

2 pounds lamb, cut into 1½-inch cubes
4 tablespoons lard
1 sm. eggplant, peeled and cut into 2-in. pieces
½ cup green beans, sliced
½ cup carrots, sliced
1 small green pepper, cut into 1-inch squares
1 small zucchini, peeled and cut into 1-inch pieces

½ pound small okra, washed and trimmed
2 medium onions, sliced
2 tomatoes, sliced
1 teaspoon salt
½ teaspoon garlic salt
1 can (4 ounces) tomato sauce
1 cup water

Brown the lamb in the lard in a large stew pan. Add all other ingredients, blending well. Cover and place in a 350-degree oven for two hours. Add a bit of water from time to time, if necessary. When meat is tender, serve immediately.

CHARLOTTE AMALIE (Serves 4)

A native alley-way restaurant in Charlotte Amalie on the U.S. Virgin Island of St. Thomas served us a delicious seafood stew we were unable to find elsewhere. What alley? Well, we can't remember, because everything in Charlotte Amalie is up an alley.

1 pound cooked lobster tail meat
1 dozen small canned clams
1 quart milk
2 whole bay leaves
3 ribs celery, chopped
4 slices lean bacon, diced
1 stick butter

2 medium onions, sliced thin
¼ cup flour
1 pint clam juice
1/8 teaspoon cayenne pepper
¼ teaspoon paprika
Salt and pepper to taste
¼ cup parsley, chopped

Cut lobster meat into large pieces. Drain clams and set to one side. Save juice. Pour milk into large pot or Dutch oven. Add bay leaves, celery, and bacon. Cover and simmer gently for ten minutes.

Melt butter in another pot and sauté onion until soft. Stir in flour. Cook and stir for two minutes. Add clam juice a bit at a time, then gradually stir in the milk. When smooth, add the clams, lobster meat, cayenne pepper, paprika, and the salt and pepper to taste. Bring to boiling point. Cook for two minutes very gently. Serve in large soup bowls and garnish with parsley.

A few years ago we were served a semi-Oriental, semi-Irish stew with dumplings in the dining room of the Hotel Filipinas in old Manila. This is it, and please notice that the mashed anchovies provide a most unusual lift.

1 cup flour
1½ teaspoons salt
2 egg yolks
1 tablespoon water
1 pound ground pork
½ pound ground ham
6 anchovies, drained and mashed
½ teaspoon pepper

6 green onions, chopped
3 cloves garlic, minced
1 can (4 ounces) water chestnuts, chopped
3 tablespoons cooking oil
2 medium onions, chopped
4 beef bouillon cubes, dissolved in 6 cups boiling water

First make dumplings. Sift flour and one-fourth teaspoon of salt into a bowl. Work in egg yolks and water with a fork. Knead until smooth and elastic. Cover bowl and let stand thirty minutes. Mix the pork, ham, anchovies, pepper, green onions, garlic, water chestnuts and remaining salt. Roll out dough on a floured board until paper thin. Cut the dough into three-inch squares. Put a teaspoon of the meat mixture in the center of each dough square and fold over in a triangle. Seal edges with egg yolk (you will have some meat left over). Heat oil in a large pot and cook onions until soft. Add remaining meat and cook and stir five minutes. Stir in the bouillon and bring to a boil. Carefully drop dumplings into the bouillon. Cover pot and simmer fifteen minutes. Add a little salt, if needed, and serve in large soup bowls.

BUENOS AIRES *(Serves 6)*

One looks back on misery almost with pleasure. And so it is a pleasure to share this recipe which made the stew which fed the drovers who participated in that agonizing ten-mile ride over the pampas.

3 pounds beef, cut into 1½-inch cubes
1 tablespoon salt
½ teaspoon pepper
1 teaspoon cinnamon
1/3 cup olive oil
12 tiny white onions, peeled

3 beef bouillon cubes, dissolved
  in 2 cups boiling water
1 can (8 ounces) tomato sauce
1 small eggplant, peeled and.diced
2 green peppers, sliced thin
½ cup raw (not instant) rice

Sprinkle beef cubes with two teaspoons of salt, pepper, and cinnamon. Heat one-fourth cup of the oil in a large pot or Dutch oven and brown the beef on all sides. Remove beef cubes to a warm platter and keep warm. Put remaining oil into the pot and cook onions until they are golden. Return the meat and add one-half cup of the bouillon and the tomato sauce. Cover and simmer for one and one-fourth hours. Heat remaining olive oil in a skillet and saute the eggplant for ten minutes, stirring to keep from burning. Sprinkle on the remaining salt and then put the eggplant into the pot with the meat. Add pepper slices, rice, and the remaining bouillon. Cover and simmer thirty minutes, and serve immediately.

Here's an adaptation of the stew we tasted in a Vei-Shou in Hong Kong. The bok choy and the Chinese egg noodles are delicious.

½ pound Chinese egg noodles
2 stalks bok choy, chopped
2 cups water
8 dried mushrooms, soaked ½ hour, drained, and cut in half
4 cups canned chicken broth

1 can (8 ounces) bamboo shoots, sliced
½ pound Chinese roast pork, sliced
1½ teaspoons soy sauce
¼ teaspoon pepper
5 green onions, chopped

Cook noodles five minutes in a large pot of water. Drain and put into a serving bowl and keep warm. Do the same with the bok choy.

Put the two cups of water into a large pot. Bring to boil, add mushrooms, and cook for five minutes. Add chicken broth and bring to a boil. Reduce heat and keep soup warm.

Arrange the bamboo shoots, bok choy, and pork slices on top of the noodles. Pour the soup over all. Add soy sauce and pepper. Garnish with the green onions and serve at once.

NOTE: Bok choy (similar to celery) can be purchased at most supermarkets, otherwise in oriental groceries. The Chinese roast pork also must be purchased at an oriental grocery.

ISTANBUL *(Serves 6)*

We found this one in a restaurant at the "new city" end of the Galata Bridge in old Istanbul. Eating, we watched a minor revolution occur on the street below, caused by a tiny scratch when two autos scarcely grazed each other on the bridge.

1 cup raw lentils
3 tablespoons olive oil
3 pounds beef, cut into 1½-inch cubes
2 medium onions, chopped
2 cloves garlic, minced

4 beef bouillon cubes, dissolved in 3 cups boiling water
1½ teaspoons salt
¼ teaspoon pepper
¼ teaspoon oregano

Wash lentils. Cover with boiling water and set aside to soak. Heat olive oil in a large pot or Dutch oven and brown beef quickly on all sides. Add onions and cook and stir until onions become soft. Add garlic, bouillon, salt, and pepper. Bring to a boil. Reduce heat, cover, and simmer for one hour. Drain the soaking lentils and add to the meat, along with the oregano. Cook, covered, another thirty minutes (until meat and lentils are tender). Add a little more salt, if necessary, and serve immediately.

(Serves 6) # HAIFA

Israel is not all commandos and C-rations. There is great dining going on there, too, as this recipe from a bustling seaport town at the foot of Mt. Carmel proves.

*3 pounds lamb,
cut into 1½-inch cubes
3 tablespoons flour
½ teaspoon pepper
1 tablespoon salt
2 tablespoons olive oil
3 medium onions, sliced thin*

*2 cloves garlic, minced
3 medium tomatoes, cut into cubes
¼ teaspoon dried ground red peppers
1 cup boiling water
1½ pounds string beans, cleaned and
cut into 2-inch lengths*

Toss the lamb in a paper bag with the flour, pepper, and salt. Heat oil in a large pot or Dutch oven and brown the lamb on all sides. Add the onions and cook slowly until soft. Pour off the olive oil. Add garlic, tomatoes, red peppers, and the cup of boiling water. Bring to boil. Reduce heat, cover, and simmer for one hour. Add the beans. Cover and cook another thirty minutes (until meat and beans are tender). Serve immediately with rice.

MALMO *(Serves 5)*

Across the Oresund from ever-popular Copenhagen is the Swedish maritime and industrial city of Malmo, Sweden, where a little stint of restaurant hopping uncovered this delicious lamb stew.

2 pounds lamb, cut into 1½-inch cubes
6 medium potatoes, sliced
6 carrots, grated
1 head cabbage, shredded
2 teaspoons salt

1 teaspoon pepper
1 tablespoon flour
2 beef bouillon cubes, dissolved in 1 cup boiling water

Place layers of the meat, potatoes, carrots, and cabbage in a large, oven-proof casserole, sprinkling the salt, pepper, and flour on each layer. Pour the bouillon over all. Cover and slip into a 325-degree oven for three hours, and serve.

(Serves 6) HEIDELBERG

Easy to make, easier to add to, here is the beginning of the Perpetual Stew that saved a family from going broke.

1 pound beef
1 pound pork
1 pound lamb
2 large onions, chopped
3 beef bouillon cubes, dissolved
in 1½ cups boiling water

1 teaspoon allspice
1 bay leaf, crumbled
½ teaspoon ginger
2 teaspoons salt
¼ teaspoon pepper

Cut beef, pork, and lamb into one and one-half inch cubes. Put everything into a large pot or Dutch oven. Bring to boil. Reduce heat, cover, and simmer two hours (until meat is tender). Serve, save the leftovers, and add something new to the stew tomorrow.

LISBON *(Serves 4)*

We found this one in the storied Alfalma section of Lisbon, home for centuries of the Moors who used to rule Portugal. Most likely it is one of the oldest stew recipes in this book.

1 cup dry red Portuguese wine
1 tablespoon salt
1½ quarts water
1 pound lean beef, cut into 1½-inch cubes
¼ pound bacon, diced
4 potatoes, peeled and quartered
5 carrots, sliced

2 or 3 turnips, peeled and quartered
1 small head cabbage, quartered
1 smoked sausage, sliced
1 cup uncooked minute rice
2 tablespoons cornstarch, dissolved in some of the stew broth

Put wine, salt, and one and one half quarts water into a large pot. Add beef and the bacon, and bring to a boil. Reduce heat, cover, and cook slowly for two hours. Add potatoes, carrots, turnips, and cabbage. When these are half-cooked, add the sliced sausage.

Remove one cup of the broth and cook the rice separately in it. Serve rice in separate dishes.

Add the diluted cornstarch, if necessary to thicken. Ladle into large serving dish, and serve hot.

(Serves 6) KOENIGSBERG

We never reached this famous Hanseatic city in East Prussia, now called Kalingrad, but its Koenigsberger Klops recipe has traveled widely, and we ran into it in West Berlin.

1½ pounds ground beef
½ pound ground veal
¾ cup dry bread crumbs
1 cup parsley, finely chopped
3 eggs
½ teaspoon salt
1½ quarts water
2 chicken bouillon cubes

1 bouquet garni (1 bay leaf, 2 red chili peppers, 10 whole peppercorns, 1 teaspoon allspice, and 4 cloves, all tied in a piece of cheesecloth)
2 lemons (remove rind and slice)
3 egg yolks, mixed with 3 tablespoons flour and a bit of water to make a smooth paste
2 tablespoons capers, drained

Chop and mix the beef, veal, bread crumbs, parsley, eggs and salt. Form balls two and one half inches in diameter. To do this, sprinkle flour in palm of one hand and roll meat in it. Drop balls into one and one half quarts of boiling water in a six-quart kettle. Water should just cover meatballs. Once water begins to boil again, drop in bouillon cubes and bouquet garni and cook slowly. After five minutes, drop in lemon rind and lemon slices. Cook twenty-five minutes. Remove lemon rind and bouquet garni. Stir a bit of broth into egg yolk-flour mixture to heat it, then stir into the pot. Add capers and season to taste. Cook five minutes more. If you desire a thicker gravy, mix a bit of cornstarch in a little water and stir into pot. Simmer until it thickens. Serve with small boiled potatoes.

VIENNA *(Serves 4)*

The Austrians have a beef stew that is every bit as delicious as those we know in America. Here is one we found in a restaurant somewhere in Vienna's first ring.

1½ pounds beef, cut into 2-inch cubes
4 tablespoons lard
5 medium-sized onions
1 teaspoon paprika
1 tablespoon vinegar
1½ teaspoons caraway seeds

1 teaspoon marjoram
2 beef bouillon cubes
1 teaspoon salt
1½ cups water
1 tablespoon flour

Cut meat and discard excess fat. Heat lard in a large pot. Slice onions into thin rings and sauté slowly, until soft and slightly yellow. Put beef cubes into the pot and add paprika, vinegar, caraway seeds, marjoram, bouillon cubes, and salt. Add water and stir to combine well. Bring to boil. Reduce heat, cover, and simmer for one and one half hours, or until meat is tender. Mix flour with a little of the gravy and stir into pot. Cook a few minutes to thicken, and serve hot.

This should be served with broad noodles. It's also good with tiny potatoes. And don't forget a bottle of good red wine.

OTHER BEST-SELLING P/S/S COOKBOOKS ARE:

THE CHOCOLATE COOKBOOK
THE CHILI COOKBOOK
THE COFFEE COOKBOOK
THE RUM COOKBOOK
COOKING FOR ORGIES AND OTHER LARGE PARTIES
THE NEW CELEBRITY COOKBOOK
THE GOLFER'S COOKBOOK

They are available wherever books are sold,
or they may be ordered directly from the
publisher. For complete list, write:

PRICE / STERN / SLOAN
Publishers, Inc., Los Angeles
410 North La Cienega Boulevard,
Los Angeles, California 90048

Johnrae Earl covers the restaurant beat for CHICAGO TODAY and also is that newspaper's resident gourmet editor. Among the hundreds of thousands of words he has written on food, restaurants, and his eternal world travels, are ten books for readers of his weekly column "Wife's Night Out."

James McCormick also is a newspaperman. He has written food and drink columns for national magazines, a definitive essay on wine, a novel, "Bravo," short stories, travel articles, and is presently working on a ballet. Earl and McCormick are also authors of Price/Stern/Sloan's "The Chili Cookbook."